# Mind Body and Spirit as a Career

# Mind Body and Spirit as a Career

*The Essential Career and Business Guide
for Mind, Body and Spirit Practitioners*

**Sasha Fenton
and
Jan Budkowski**

## Zambezi Publishing Ltd

First published in 2024 in the UK by Zambezi Publishing Ltd
Plymouth, Devon PL2 2EQ
Tel: +44 (0)1752 367 300
email: zambezipub@gmail.com     www.zampub.com

British Library Cataloguing in Publication Data:
A catalogue record for this book is available from the British Library

ISBN(13) 978-1-915176-02-8
Illustrations & cover image:
copyright © 2024 Jan Budkowski
Typesetting by Zambezi Publishing Ltd, Plymouth

Advisory note: all images apart from author photos
have been created with the help of AI resources.
All text has been written without using AI.

Disclaimer:- This book is intended to provide general information
regarding the subject matter, and to entertain. The contents are not
exhaustive and no warranty is given as to accuracy of content. The book
is sold on the understanding that neither the publisher nor the author
are thereby engaged in rendering professional services, in respect of the
subject matter or any other field. If expert guidance is required, the
services of a qualified professional should be sought.
Readers are urged to access a range of other material on the book's
subject matter, and to tailor the information to their individual needs.
Neither the author nor the publisher shall have any responsibility to any
person or entity regarding any loss or damage caused or alleged to be
caused, directly or indirectly, by the use or misuse of information
contained in this book. If you do not wish to be bound by the above,
you may return this book in original condition to the publisher, with its
receipt, for a refund of the purchase price.

# About the Authors

## Sasha Fenton

*Media*

Sasha wrote the stars page for Woman's Own magazine for six years and for the Sunday People for two years, along with over 3,000 articles and columns for papers and magazines. She has broadcast on most British radio stations and many TV shows, usually about Astrology and other Mind, Body & Spirit (MB&S) subjects.

*Organisations*

Former member of the Executive Council of the Writers' Guild of Great Britain
Former member of the British Astrological & Psychic Society (BAPS)
Member and former Committee member of the Federation of Small Businesses.
Twice Organiser of Plymouth Small Business Saturday.

*Books*

Sasha has written 142 books, mostly published by a number of mainstream publishers including Thorsons, HarperCollins, Carlton, Piatkus, Sterling Publishing Inc.,and currently Quarto Publishing Group USA Inc.

*Zambezi Publishing Ltd*

Sasha and her husband, Jan Budkowski, started Zambezi Publishing Ltd (Zampub) in 1998. Zampub has produced over 300 books, mainly in the MB&S genre, including the prestigious "Simply" series and the current "In Focus" series. Many of our titles have also been co-published with larger publishers.

*Stellium Ltd*

Stellium offers high quality traditional fiction and non-fiction publishing and self-publishing services, along with popular ebook products. In today's incredibly difficult publishing environment, self-publishing has become virtually the only entry point for authors that may subsequently lead to adoption by a mainstream publisher.

# Jan Budkowski

Jan Budkowski was born to Polish parents in Lusaka, Zambia. After a fulfilling childhood and receiving a quality education, he embarked on a career in banking. Over the course of 31 years, he progressed to an executive role within the same bank, while moving from Zambia to South Africa.

Upon relocating to the UK, Jan shifted his focus to writing and publishing. Over the past twenty eight years, Jan and his wife, Sasha Fenton, have published numerous books covering a range of topics including mind, body and spirit, health and business subjects. Jan's deep-rooted interest in psychology, astrology, and ancient mythology sparked his fascination with the Runes and their applications in counselling and forecasting, leading to him writing In Focus: Runes for Quarto Group, USA.

His extensive background in banking and publishing equip him with the necessary business acumen for a project of this nature. Furthermore, his experience in interacting with individuals from various walks of life provides him with the practical insight required to understand the unique requirements of those involved in the mind, body, and spirit realm.

Jan and his astrologer wife, Sasha Fenton, live in Devon and enjoy being in this beautiful part of the country. His hobbies include archery, fly fishing and photography.

# Contents

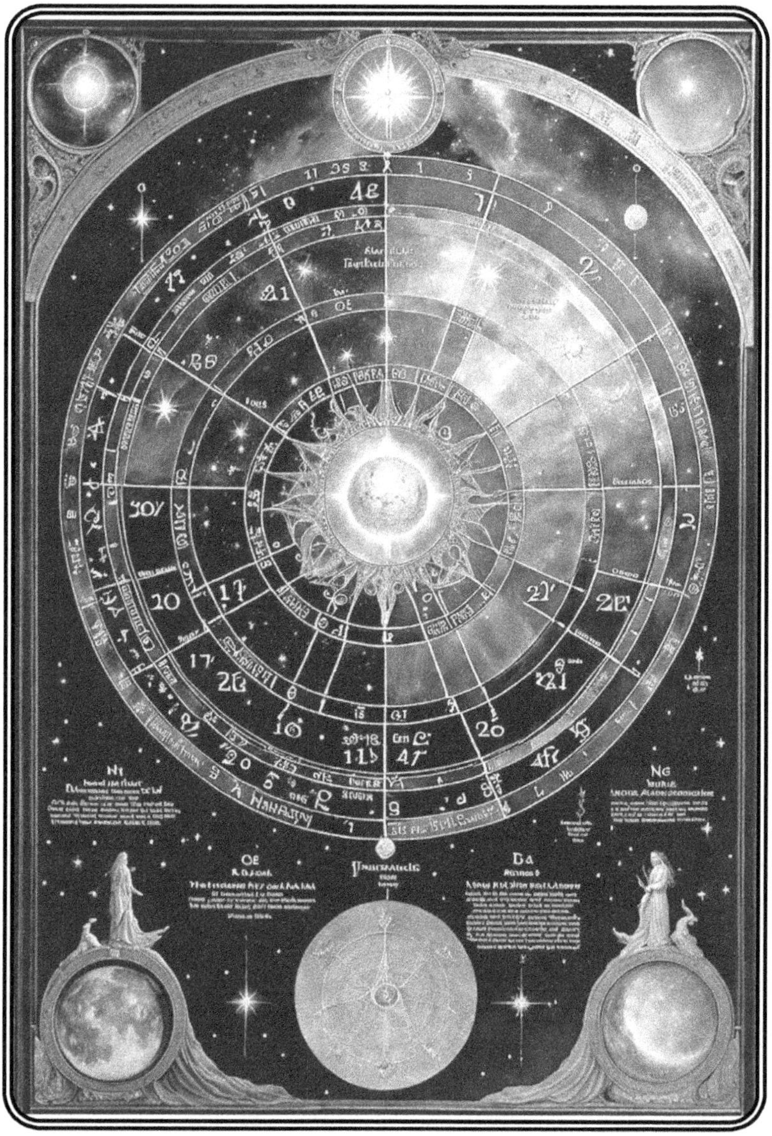

# 1: The Basics

## Who is This Book For?

This book is for anyone who gives readings, works as a healer or therapist, or wishes to do so. It applies to those who want to earn a full or part-time living, or raise money for charity. The information applies whether you wish to do this kind of work for the rest of your life or only for a short period. We have tried to cover various needs and viewpoints, but this book is about the business and practical issues involved in the wider Mind, Body and Spirit field. It is primarily intended to help those who want to make a full or part-time living from a consultancy.

Your motivation for giving readings or healing may primarily be spiritual. You may have financial resources enabling you to have no desire or real need to earn money, and you may even feel it is wrong for you to do so. If so, you will still find much in this book to show you how to succeed in what you do. If you need to earn money, as most of us do, we will show you how to give your clients quality service while at the same time enjoying a decent income from the fruits of your efforts.

## *Technology*

When we wrote the first version of this book two decades ago, the internet was in its infancy; many people had yet to learn to use a computer - let alone email - while mobile phones only made phone calls; video connections by mobile phone only existed in science fiction. Now you can work at a distance via Zoom, Skype or your mobile phone; even palmists use snapshots sent to their mobile phones. Technology constantly changes, so you must always keep yourself updated.

### Marketing

In any business, whether it be manufacturing, selling goods or giving a service, you need to bring your "product" to the notice of the public. Marketing is the key to building a clientele, and we can give you some ideas on how to do this.

### A Day's Work for a Day's Pay

Being self-employed requires far more self-motivation than going out to work. If you work in a proper job, you may have targets to meet and budgets to keep within, but when you are self-employed, you must become your own supervisor, manager and slave driver. If you only want to work for a few hours each week, that's fair enough, but if you want to make a living, you will have to put in at least the same hours that you would in a regular job, and maybe more.

Be enthusiastic about your work, keep your eyes on the stars and make it happen. Ensure that you have a good "product" and market it well. Keep working and build for the future, learn from your mistakes and save some of your income for quiet times. Keep a positive mental attitude and even your own Spiritual guides will become excited by your progress. If you are negative, lazy, uninspired or boring, they will find someone else to channel their love and inspiration through.

---

*Some of the advice and examples in this book come from Sasha, while much of the financial content comes from Jan.*

---

# 2: Starting Up

## Why Start a Small Business?

There are lots of reasons why people start small businesses, and a good way of understanding this is to watch a few episodes of Dragon's Den, where you will see hopeful people of all kinds either starting up or expanding their businesses. Fortunately, a business of our kind is not as challenging to start up as many of those that we see on that programme.

Some people who start their own businesses have a great desire to change the world, others want to become rich or famous, while yet others just want to work for themselves rather than other people. Some have an invention that they wish to market, while others have a skill they can use, such as accountancy or laying crazy paving. We who work in the mind, body and spirit world are passionate about what we do, and most of us want to help others while also making some form of income for ourselves.

The "civilian" world out there will claim that we are turning a hobby into a business. Well, so what? Some people make a living by selling model railways, mending old clocks, collecting stamps, running a surfer's shop, or creating and selling retro clothes. Even if what we do is no more than turning a hobby into a part-time income, there is nothing wrong with that. Women who work in our field are often driven by the need to find work that can fit around family life, and there is nothing wrong with that, either. As long as what we do interests others, it has a market that makes it worth doing.

### *No Age Barriers*

The world of tech is suitable for those under thirty, but our world is not dependent upon tech other than the usual stuff that is everywhere these days. Clients are comfortable with older workers who have years of experience behind them that they can bring to the job, so age is no barrier. Indeed, our work is not really suited to young people, but young people inevitably grow older, so as long as they keep learning their trade, they will soon be old enough to carry it out.

### Famous People

While thinking about unexpected people who have actually earned money from their talents, one surprising example was the Italian dictator Mussolini. Apparently, when young, he worked as a part-time Reader of some kind. I guess he must have had a talent for what he did, along with some knowledge of playing card reading, astrology or palmistry or whatever he used, because a charlatan who makes things up won't last long in our business. However, in the case of Mussolini, one has to wonder whether he predicted his own success or foresaw his horrific downfall!

### A Business Name

You can call yourself or your business practically anything you like, but choose something that expresses what you do or what you believe in without sounding silly. Then, do a Google search for that name in case there is already a business or company using the name. You can't do business copying someone else's name; it's illegal, and you could be sued. When I was a Reader, I used my first name as my business name because "Sasha" stood out enough in those days to do the trick for a sole proprietor. When Jan and I started our publishing business in 1996, we were looking for an email address that hadn't already been used, and all the planetary names or other astrology connections had gone.

I suggested we choose something African because Jan had been born and raised in Zambia near the Zambezi River, and we had spent a few days on a houseboat on the Zambezi soon after we first got together. So Jan came up with the name Zambezi, and I suggested we make it Zambezi Publishing Ltd. The name works for us because people easily remember it.

When you get to the point of having a separate bank account for your business, it will probably be a "No. 2" account, run off the back of your personal account. The cheques will have your own name followed by T/A, which means trading as, and then it will show the name of your business. When I was self-employed, my cheques said: Sasha Fenton T/A Sasha.

## *Varying Your Work*

You might be able to vary what you do. For instance, among my friends are a palmist who has become a herbalist, a yoga teacher who is also a psychic, a nutrition expert who is also an astrologer, a medium who is a Tarot reader, a Reiki healer who is also an artist and several who have written books. Not all the books are about mind, body and spirit subjects, and some are novels. Some enterprising people put on workshops or run mind, body and spirit festivals, while others do some of their work online where they can reach a wider clientele.

## *A Partial or Full Income*

Our work is probably only likely to generate a partial income, but that is fine too, as every little helps these days. Trying to make a complete living out of a Consultancy would be highly stressful, as it can't be relied upon as a means of paying the day-to-day bills. A few people do manage it, but the majority do something else as well, or have a pension or some other form of income.

## *A Business Plan*

If you need to raise capital (money) to help start your business, your bank will ask you to write a business plan or work out a forecast of what you think your business will make over the next two or three years. You will find examples of business plans online. It strikes me that business forecasts are a combination of guesswork and wishful thinking, and it also strikes me that those of us who give readings should be the best-placed people in the world when it comes to forecasting anything! Fortunately, I have never had to write a business plan or produce a financial forecast, so I suggest you also try to avoid this nightmare if you can. Like all businesses, yours will go through good and bad times and even with your MB&S skill set(s), you won't always see the bad times coming. So always keep some money in hand for those times when your business dries up for a while. You should aim to keep enough money set aside as a business reserve fund to keep you going for at least a year.

### *The Legal Structure*

The legal structure of most businesses is that of Sole Trader, Partnership or Limited Company. There are other types of legal structures, but these are the most common ones.

Sometimes people get together with a marriage-type partner or a couple of family members and start a business together – say running a restaurant – in which case they would form a Partnership, but as a Consultant, you will be a Sole Trader, if, indeed, you even need to take things that far. If you are only earning a bit of pin money by giving readings or therapy treatments to friends and neighbours, there may be no need to do anything. However, if your work becomes more than this – and especially if you are dealing with the general public – you will need to take action. As you will see later in this book, it is amazing how quickly the Department of Work and Pensions discover who is earning shady money, and they can make your life difficult - especially if you are also receiving some kind of benefit.

At the time of writing this book, if you have earned more than £1,000 during the previous tax year, you will need to register as a Sole Trader. Fortunately, all the information you need is available online, so do a Google search for the phrase: Starting a Business. If you need to make a tax return, you will have to register for self-assessment, and for this, you will need a Unique Taxpayer Reference from HM Revenue and Customs (HMRC).

Apparently, if you are self-employed, you can claim Tax-Free Childcare, so if you have children, you should look into this.

If you find this kind of thing daunting, it might be worth asking an accountant for advice; this shouldn't be expensive because you aren't asking the accountant to do your bookkeeping or anything that requires complicated work. I can remember registering as a Sole Trader many years ago, and I paid £16 for the accountant to handle the registration paperwork for me. That was a long time ago, though, so I expect it will cost much more than that now, but it could be well worth it for the confidence it gives you. You need to stay within the law, especially when money is involved.

You can definitely have a main job and have your MB&S practice as what is now called a Side Hustle, but you need to look into the tax implications. Chances are that your Side Hustle won't make any difference to your tax position at all, but you need to find out for sure.

Fortunately, there is a lot of information online and even free workshops that will show you what to do about tax and all other aspects of starting up a small enterprise. You could try YouTube for inspiration.

### *National Insurance*
One thing you really need to do is keep up your national insurance payments. It may be tempting to pay a reduced fee due to being a small earner, but this will reduce the amount you receive as your State Pension when the time comes. If, by chance, you owe a couple of years back-payment for some part of your NI, it would be worth bringing this up to date.

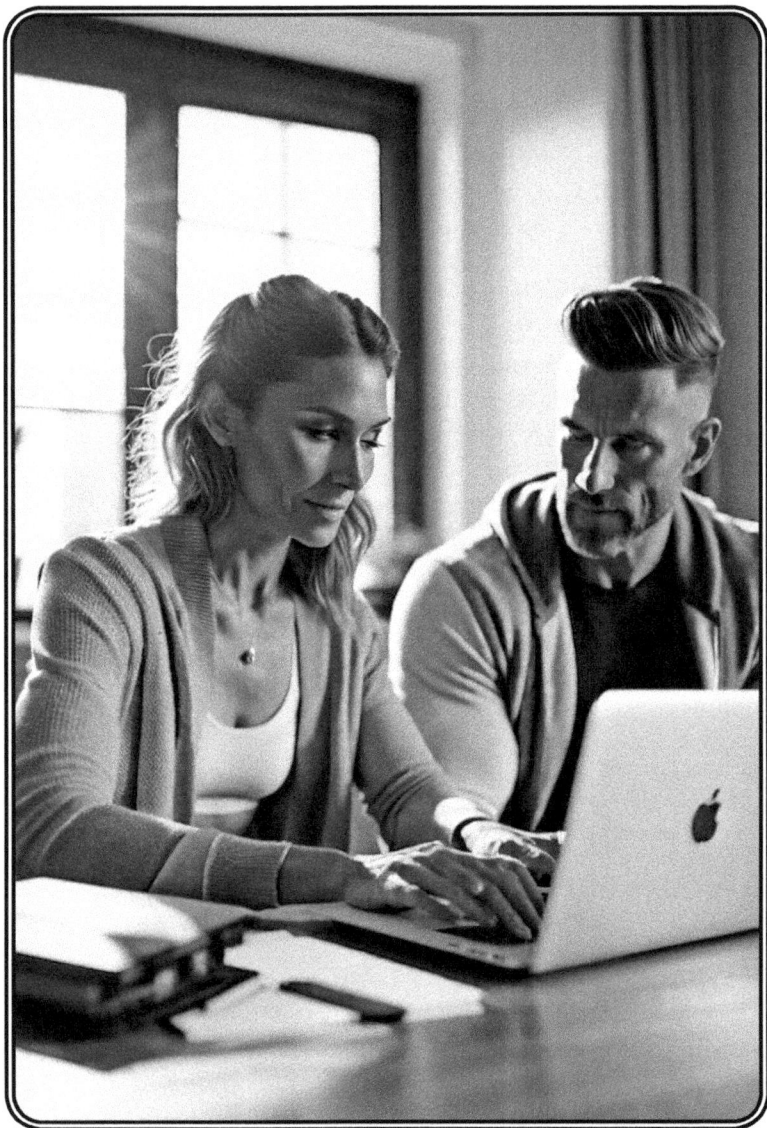

# 3: Money Matters

## *Raising Money*
Your best bet is to have a main job as well as your Consultancy and finance your own little business yourself. If this is not possible, you may wish to raise some capital (money). Here are a few ideas that might help.

## *Family and Friends*
You can check whether your partner or a family member would be happy to give or lend you something to help you get going.

A gift is great, but if the relative or friend can only *lend* money rather than give you something, you must be very professional about this. Write down the terms of the loan and the arrangements for repaying it, make two copies, and ensure that both parties sign them. Sample contracts are available by doing a Google search. That way, you will have a legal contract that benefits both of you. Don't delay or default on any of the repayments, or you will cause a great deal of aggravation to yourself and everyone else.

## *A Government Loan*
Nowadays, there are government-backed startup loans that run from £500 to £25,000, and this could be worth looking into, especially if you need to buy a vehicle. Remember that loans have to be repaid.

## *Big Ideas*
There are venture capitalists who lend money to businesses, but they deal with much larger ones than your little enterprise, and they may have terms that would not suit you. Similarly, there are "business angels" who lend money and also offer advice and mentoring, but you need to check out their terms and conditions carefully before getting involved, even assuming they would want

to lend money to a business as small as yours. If you decided to put on a large psychic fair, though… well, I guess that might interest them, provided that you could convince them of your ability to cope with such a project.

You could set up a *crowdfunding* project online. This route can be helpful, but it can be risky as well. You should thoroughly discuss the idea with an accountant before seeking funds this way.

## Small Ideas

The good news is that our type of business doesn't need much money to get going. The biggest investment will be a vehicle if you don't already have one, and you might be able to get around that by leasing one. Another biggie for a reflexologist, masseur or beautician is a treatment table. Nevertheless, there are many second-hand ones listed online, and the prices run from around £100 upwards, depending on their age and quality.

When I started up, I financed my astrology business out of my earnings, taking time to buy the various things that I needed when I could afford them. I was lucky enough to have a car, so my biggest expense was a computer and printer, but later on, I bought a tabletop photocopier and a telephone answering machine. Amazingly, even now, all these years later, while I am working as a publisher rather than as a Consultant astrologer, my office setup is much the same as it was then, and I have much the same equipment in it as I did then.

## Universal Credit

You may need to look into Universal Credit. This allows you to work a certain number of hours and earn a certain amount of money while receiving benefits, but there are stringent rules that you must look into and adhere to.

You could have a few really good weeks where you earn more money than usual, but this can reach the ears of the Universal Credit Department. If so, your Universal Credit income would very likely come to a sudden halt. The Universal Credit system doesn't realise that you are not the same as an employee who has a regular wage, and it doesn't realise that your income will fluctuate. It also doesn't realise that you will have operating costs that will reduce your income. If this benefit is stopped, the theory is that you can reapply for it, but I am not sure that actually works because if a benefit is cancelled, that may count against you in a fresh application. The message here is to watch your income and outgoings very carefully.

When Jan and I dealt with the authorities, we discovered that some people who worked there didn't understand the difference between a company's gross income and net profit. The gross income is everything that comes in *before* any bills or taxes have been paid, and the net profit is what is left *after* everything has been paid for. The officials thought that every penny that comes in belongs to the business owner, which is far from reality in a business setting!

## *Make a Business Budget*
If you are a whizz on the computer, you might set up a spreadsheet to record your money flow over time, but if not, you can do this in a notebook. As you will see, much of the following are everyday business expenses, and luckily, most of them won't apply to you.

## *Business Premises*
You will probably work from home or at occasional events, so you are unlikely to have to pay rent for your business. If you do pay some kind of rent to a place of work, you need to budget for this and build up a reserve in case your income stream drops or stops for a while.

## *A Business Vehicle*
You probably already have a vehicle that you only use for the business on occasion. However, if you sell goods, you may need a van.

## *Business Equipment*
You will definitely need a phone, and you may need a tablet or computer and a printer.

### Staff
You shouldn't need permanent staff, but a friend may help you from time to time, for whom you should do something in return.

### Setting up and Hosting a Website
This could well be something you will need to budget for, even if you are able to set up the website yourself; there are ongoing hosting costs and other expenses involved.

### Advertising and Marketing
This will definitely cost money, and not all of it will work. Business cards are essential, though.

### Specialist Equipment
There will be some expenses here, but the amount you lay out at the start of your business venture will depend upon the type of business involved. For instance, a therapist will need quite a lot of expensive equipment, while a palmist will only need printing ink, paper, a pretty table cloth and a good light. An astrologer must have a computer to produce natal charts and other information for the client.

### Festivals and Events
These will cost money, as do travel expenses, meals and overnight accommodation if the event takes up more than one day.

### Savings for Quiet Seasons
Put money aside during good times to cover your needs during slow ones. Always save at least ten per cent of your gross income in a separate reserve account; don't just leave it in your main account, or you will surely lose track and end up with a problem.

### FaceBook Groups
There may be a Facebook group devoted to budgeting, YouTube very likely has lots of guidance available, and a Google search will certainly help.

### Online Videos
Do a Google search and check YouTube as well for startup information

# 4: Your Place of Work

## Working from Home

The most obvious place for you to consider working in is your home, and while some people can now get away with working remotely by Skype, Zoom, telephone or email, therapists need a place where clients can visit them. The advantages of working from home are:

- You are already on-site, so no rent or other fees are involved.
- You can use your own phone and answering machine.
- There are no travelling expenses and no time wasted by travelling.
- Your workroom can be arranged any way you want.
- If anybody else touches your stuff, it is only likely to be a member of your own family.
- You don't have to carry your goods or equipment anywhere.
- You can have a coffee or a snack when you feel like it.
- Family arrangements such as picking up children from school are easier to arrange.
- You can work the hours and the days that suit your lifestyle.

### *Home Checklist*

Look at the checklist below to see whether your home has the right potential.

- Is your home easy to get to by public transport?
- Is your home easy to find?
- Is your home in a reasonably pleasant location?
- Is there sufficient parking close by?
- Are your neighbours supportive?

- Do you have a suitable room that you can use?
- Is your home relatively secure from thieves?
- Are you adequately insured? For theft and professional indemnity?
- Is your family setup suitable?

Your clients should be able to reach your home by public transport, and have sufficient parking space if using a car. If your home is not easy to find, you must give clear directions over the phone or even send a map to your clients beforehand. The outside appearance of your place is reasonably immaterial; however, common sense suggests that nobody will want to visit a dump, although some disadvantages can be overcome if you have a good reputation. An example is our friend, Barbara Ellen, who ran an extremely successful consultancy in a top-floor flat that could only be reached after climbing several flights of rickety iron stairs.

Any spare room can be turned into a beautiful consulting room; if you don't have an extra room and have a back garden large enough to hold a construction of some kind, this may be a possible solution. You might be able to put up a double-skinned shed or a caravan, or you may be able to convert a garage for the purpose.

## Food and Drink
You are not running a cafe, so you don't need to do anything for your clients other than give them a reading, healing session or therapy. However, if the appointment is likely to take some time, you may wish to make your client comfortable by offering them a drink and maybe a biscuit, especially if you fancy something yourself. If the day is hot, always offer your client a cold drink.

## Smoking and Drinking
I was a smoker many years ago, and many people in my field also smoked, as did many of my clients, but those days are long gone, so even if someone wants to smoke, don't allow them to do so in your premises. Put up a clear notice to this effect. In fact, business premises are forbidden by law to allow smoking.

Never drink alcohol when working, whether at home, at a festival, or any other location. Alcohol does not improve your abilities; it lessens them. Furthermore, if your clients smell drink on you, you soon won't have any clients left, and if you are seen drinking at a festival, the organisers may throw you out.

### *Your Loo*

One Reader who I knew used her downstairs hallway as a waiting room, and she had several well-made plastic signs artfully placed on her stairs showing prices and details about her readings. The best sign of all proclaimed in large letters that using her loo was strictly forbidden! Fortunately, this Reader lived just off a busy high street, and a public loo was nearby.

Using your own lavatory is an important matter to consider; believe it or not, it's tricky. Many clients will have come quite a long way to see you, and they may need the loo, while others are nervous, affecting their bladders. It would be churlish not to allow them to relieve themselves, but be careful how you arrange this; if you have a downstairs loo close to your office, this is fine, but if your clients must run upstairs or wander unsupervised through your house, you may have a problem. In such a case, ensure that inner doors are closed and, if possible, locked. Clients can be light-fingered; you don't want them to steal anything or assess your premises for a future break-in. Obviously, you must keep your toilet clean and hygienic, and ensure sufficient toilet paper is available, but you don't need to provide a bin for sanitary towels. People being what they are, you can expect "accidents" of one kind or another, especially if they bring children, so don't be surprised if you need to disinfect the toilet on occasion.

### *Clients with Children*

If your client brings a child with them, common sense will also dictate how you deal with this. Small children often sit with their mothers, while older ones can be sent to your waiting area and given a magazine to read. If you know and trust your client, you might even allow a youngster to sit in another room and watch your television.

### *Your Waiting Area*

This is another surprisingly tricky situation, and I have even known Readers who won't allow a client who arrives early to enter their premises. Having a specific room to work in is a luxury for most consultants, but having a waiting room as well is often out of the question. I had a conservatory and some nice garden chairs in one of my previous homes, which was a terrific place for my clients. At other times, I have allowed them to sit in my living room, and my family often had their company while watching the TV, but years later, my children told me that many of these people bored them witless by plying them with questions about me and my work.

## *Insurance*
You need to insure the contents of your home, but you also need Public Liability insurance for yourself and Professional Indemnity insurance. These are not too expensive, but do an internet search to find something that suits you. One reasonably priced, reliable source is currently available via our sister company, MBS Professionals Ltd, with a discount for Readers who qualify for membership of this professional organisation. Visit www.mbsprofessionals.com for information about the organisation, and contact us for insurance application details at mbsprofessionals@gmail.com

## *Loneliness*
If you live alone, spending too much time at home can make you lonely, isolated and even agoraphobic! You may have clients dancing in and out of your place hour after hour, but they are not your friends! Clients come to see you because they need a reading, and some will decide you are their friend - mainly because you are the only person interested in their problems. Some clients may eventually become personal friends; still, the number is likely to be very small indeed, so even though you will meet many people during your working day, you can become very lonely!

For this reason, it is worth considering doing some of your readings outside the home and in the company of other Readers. A weekend at a psychic fair - especially if this is away from home - allows you to mix with others in the same line as yourself and spend time "talking shop" and trading useful information. This kind of networking is often a vital part of any job, so if you can do this occasionally, it will recharge your psychic batteries. Try to have a social life or hobbies that take you out of your home if possible, as this will lessen feelings of isolation.

Oddly enough, if you don't get out into the real world frequently enough, you can eventually become afraid to do so! Try to leave your house for a while every day if you can, even if only to pop out to the shops for a pint of milk, because this could save your sanity. One final idea that my husband, Jan, suggests is to put up a few mirrors here and there in the house, as seeing yourself reflected in them will make you feel less isolated.

## *Other Locations*
Not everybody's home circumstances are conducive to home working, so let us look at some alternatives. Even those who can work from home occasionally fancy a change of scene, and you may wish to take advantage of alternatives. The following list may help:

- A friend's house.
- A local shop.
- Psychic or wellbeing fairs.
- Telephone, postal, Skype or email readings.
- Party-plan healing, treatment or readings.
- Hotels, pubs, clubs, restaurants, formal office parties.
- A psychic centre, a holistic centre, a complementary health centre.

## *Someone Else's Home*
You may have a friend who has a vacant room and is happy to allow you to work from their premises in return for an agreed fee or a percentage of what you make from your work. If you can't take bookings yourself, your friend may be able to do this for you, which means that you will have some clients lined up in advance.

If you haven't read through the chapter on working from home, do so now because most of our covered points will apply. For example, the accessibility of the location and the safety factor if you expect to be alone in the house.

## *A Local Shop*

You might contact a local shop that sells goods complementary to your work, to see whether they would rent you a corner to work from. You can pay for your space on a straightforward rental basis, meaning that you and the shop know exactly what this will amount to, or you can give a percentage of the takings. The shopkeeper could display a permanent notice in the window as this will bring in enquiries, whether you are present or not. If the shop takes bookings for you, this means that you will have at least some of your hours accounted for before you arrive for your day's work, but bear in mind that the shopkeeper is more likely to take an interest in booking people for you if he is on a percentage of your takings. Also remember that if the shop gets busy, the last thing the shop staff will want to be bothered with is making bookings for you.

Bookings are one thing, but you should never allow someone else to take actual money for you. Your colleagues may be honest and wonderful bookkeepers and record keepers, but we have had the experience of messy bookkeeping (and worse), and you don't need to give away any of your precious income in this way. It is hard enough to earn a living without suffering losses by accident or on purpose.

These days, you will have a mobile phone, which means you can make your bookings whether you are actually at the shop or not. This will give you flexibility and control of your clients and your income. A few clients will turn up unannounced, hoping to be able to see you, and that may be fine too.

It is not worth approaching a bustling shop; they won't need or want you there. While a reasonably quiet venue won't bring you much passing trade, it could be useful if you make most of your bookings by phone. On the other hand, if there is no trade at all or the place is in an awkward location, it won't be of any use. A friend of mine once rented space at a dead-loss antiques market and found this to be a total waste of time, money and energy.

One thing you can't do is work in the street or any other public place unless it is at a specific mind, body and spirit event, as it is illegal to do so.

## *Psychic Fairs and Festivals*

Psychic fairs and festivals are worth considering, sometimes not so much for the money you might make as for the opportunity to hand out business cards and leaflets about yourself and your services. Psychic fairs vary greatly in size, scope and effectiveness, but the large ones may be out of your league due to the cost of renting a stand. Events differ tremendously, as do the stand rental charges and the footfall that comes through the door. You can find out what Readers charge at such events by visiting one yourself and looking around. In our experience, there is an optimum fee that the Readers at the fair will charge, but this can differ from fair to fair. If you rent a stand, you should take a fibre-tipped pen, some card and perhaps a plastic stencil set to make up a suitable notice on the spot.

Fairs are excellent training grounds, even for an experienced Reader, because you must deal with whoever shows up for a reading and cope with noise and other distractions. If you try your hand at fairs, ensure you have plenty of business cards, leaflets and other literature, as such give-outs are an excellent source of future business. Think carefully before agreeing to take space at a fair that is too far away, as the cost of travel and accommodation will significantly reduce your profit. However, if the fair is known to be well run and attended, it may still be worth doing.

If you have anything tangible to sell, it can add interest to your stand. However, this becomes a two-handed venture because it's impossible to concentrate on readings or giving treatment and selling goods simultaneously. If you are selling anything of value, you absolutely must have someone else on the stand to look after your stock and prevent it from "walking" off the stand.

If you enjoy teaching or demonstrating your skills, you can offer to give a talk. This is always useful, as a few audience members will likely come to your stand for a reading or a treatment after your talk. Never be pushed into giving the last talk of the day because there will be no time to cash in on this or speak to anyone afterwards. Once again, if you give a talk, ensure that you provide a leaflet or business card with your details to each person who comes in. Remember that if you must leave your stand to give a lecture or for any other reason, you must have someone on hand to guard your possessions. Perhaps a nearby stallholder will be willing to reciprocate the help.

You can often rent a large enough space for two or three people to share. This helps you deal with the abovementioned problems and can be more cost-effective than renting an individual stand. Going with a friend means sharing expenses and perhaps travelling together to and from the event. It also means you have someone to chat with during slack moments.

### *Distant Services*

You may give Tarot readings, advice on life-coaching or nutrition or even lessons by phone, Skype, Zoom and so on, and these methods can be very useful, as you don't have to put up with people tramping in and out of your home, and you don't have to go anywhere either. If a client contacts you, they may expect you to give them what they want there and then, but you must make it clear that you need to be paid in advance by direct payment into a bank account or by credit card, PayPal, SumUp or a similar service. You must look into all these methods and choose at least one that best suits your needs. If you use a bank account for people to pay into, keep it separate from your personal accounts, and always ensure that it has very little money in it. That way, if a criminal manages to hack into the account, they can only steal the few pounds you leave there. There are card payment devices to deal with credit cards and other payment methods, and these can all be useful, so you need to investigate what is available.

You must enjoy this kind of work, or you won't give the best of readings, and you'll end up giving money back to your clients if they are dissatisfied. On the other hand, everyone has an occasional failure, so accept that an occasional refund may be required.

Your clients need to know that they must make the phone call, as this can't land on your phone bill, but Skype and Zoom cost little or nothing for the caller to use. Even though this kind of work is cost-effective, your time is valuable, so you may wish to keep sessions within an allotted time - usually no longer than one hour.

Remote work can suit graphologists and astrologers who work on a scientific vibration rather than a psychic one, and it suits advisors of all kinds. It can also suit psychics who are happy to hold a photograph of the client, and this can be done quite easily using a mobile phone. Even palmists work this way now, with the client sending a palm print by phone before the reading starts.

## *Postal Services*

I seriously suggest that you avoid doing charts or written or packaged readings for any third party. Someone may decide that a packaged reading would be just the right birthday present for their friend or as a thank you to someone who has done them a favour. Suppose you can supply a commercial, computerised horoscope report package or something similar. In that case, this is fine because these products are all pretty vague and innocuous, but a "real" reading is different. I sincerely feel that readings should be requested by the person who wants one. What do you say if you discover that the recipient of this "gift" has a truly lousy year ahead of him? Do you lie? Do you tell all? The whole scenario gives me goose pimples. Worse still, someone who hasn't requested a reading, therapy, healing or specialist advice won't value it.

## *Party Plan Sessions*

One rather pleasant way of working is when someone (usually a woman) asks a few friends round and then employs you as the reader for the evening; you can approach this in various ways. Firstly, you may give a little talk to the assembled company followed by a few readings, or you can simply make yourself comfortable in another room and deal with one client after another. You will need to work out a reasonable time scale for the job and an affordable price for each reading, and you may decide to give the hostess a freebee reading as part of the package. These days most people expect to have their reading recorded, so they might want to bring their mobiles along to record your words. Party-plan reading is hard work but enjoyable, because the clients are in a mild form of party mode. When you have finished your evening's work, you will doubtless be able to have a drink, a snack and a chat with the party clients.

Your readings will need to be relatively short and sweet, so you will doubtless charge less than you would if each client visited your home separately, but this usually turns out to be worth the effort from a financial point of view. Ensure there will be a sensible number of clients for the job because too few make the trip a waste of time. At the same time, too many means that you will sit in your party-planner's house until three in the morning, or some people will leave disappointed.

I can think of two drawbacks to this kind of work, with the first being that you might have difficulty finding the location, especially as the night in question will inevitably be dark, wet and dismal. The other is that it is quite tiring as you will do several readings, one after the other.

### Other Exotic Venues

Don't turn your nose up at the idea of giving readings at your local school's fete. Sitting in a tent for an afternoon doing quick readings and then giving the money you earn to the school for its own use may not appear to be a great commercial success. Still, it offers a magnificent opportunity to dish out business cards and leaflets. If the school is near your home or business, the spin-off from this can be excellent. It also benefits from being a buzzy location with happy people around. As you are likely to be the only Reader or therapist there, you won't have the kind of competition you have at any psychic fair.

I have done readings at radio stations, newspaper offices, employment agencies and all manner of dinner dances. Sometimes I have been the only Reader present, and sometimes there have been a few of us dotted around the place. One Halloween evening, I was even given a witch's hat to wear! As it happened, I didn't need this, as I always take my own witchy hat along to any Halloween occasion.

The late John Lindsay and I had a lovely little job in a nightclub which we did once a month for about two years. The nightclub's management paid us a set fee for each night's work, so we never had to worry about the number of clients likely to turn up. As it happens, we were always packed out from the moment we arrived until the club shut in the early hours of the following morning. The clients paid nothing for their readings as we were part of the "entertainment" put on by the club.

Hotels and other public places such as restaurants might be happy to organise an event. You may be the only Reader on hand, or the affair could be something much more ambitious, such as three or four consultants, each offering a different kind of reading. Some hotels are happy to put on a weekend event during their off-season as this brings in business for them. Such an event can include lectures, demonstrations and readings.

If you have a flair for organisation and enough salesmanship and sheer chutzpah to get a hotel involved in such a scheme, it could work well and even become a regular event. I remember that in the case of the one I attended, I was paid a set fee for my lectures and then a percentage of the fees they charged for my readings. A treasurer handled all the bookings, details and money, but I kept a note of what I had done to ensure that it tallied with what I was paid after the event. It worked just fine.

## Readings in the Workplace
Some people give readings at their place of work during their lunch hour, and while this can be a fun thing to do occasionally and it can generate useful interest in your product, this method of working has its drawbacks. There is more against this than for it, so I don't recommend it.

## The Travelling Reader
Our friend Barbara Ellen is a psychic who has now retired, but she travelled the world for many years with her work. Barbara arranged for a local person in the country she was due to work in to advertise before her arrival that she would be in town and to arrange advance bookings for her. Barbara arrived, worked through a list of clients for several days, stopped working, socialised, saw the sights, and generally enjoyed being wherever she was. Barbara went around the world several times by this means, working in different parts of America, Japan, Malta, Hong Kong, Hawaii and just about everywhere else. She even worked in the UK from time to time. If you enjoy travelling, this is a neat way of doing it.

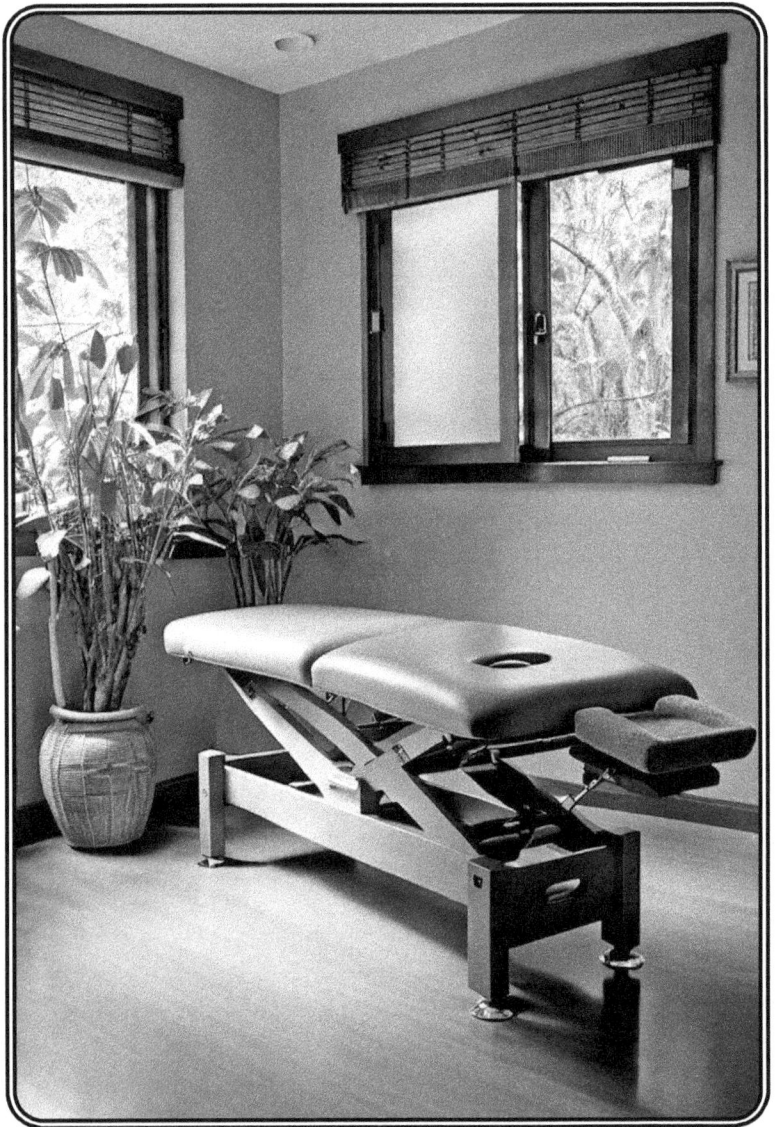

# 5: Startup Equipment

Assuming that you want to work from home, there will be expenses to plan for. You don't have to buy everything in one go because you can equip yourself as time goes by. You could also consider asking friends and relatives to buy some items for you for Christmas or your birthday.

The main thing is to keep receipts for everything you buy and list your expenses, perhaps in a spreadsheet or, at the very least, in a notebook. When listing these items, record the date you bought each item, what it was and how much it cost. Later in this book, we will look into bookkeeping in more detail.

Here are a few ideas, although your specific needs will depend upon what you do, and they will evolve over time.

## *Items for Readings*
- A table and a fancy cloth to go over it.
- Tarot and other cards, runes, crystals or other tools of the trade.
- A laptop computer or tablet and software for astrology, numerology readings, etc.
- A mobile phone or landline that can take messages.
- A digital MP3 voice recorder (and player). Record the session and send the client their copy as an email attachment. Get one that uses AA or AAA batteries (take spare batteries). Or, if the one you like is a rechargeable model, make sure to take a portable charger along, because these gadgets always run out of charge at the wrong time!
- If you are a palmist, you will need a good light and the equipment for taking handprints, or for remote readings, you may ask your clients to photograph their hands on their mobiles and send the images to you for analysis.

- You may want candles, music on a digital MP3 player, incense and pot plants.
- Software, especially for astrology.

## *Items for Therapies*

- A therapy table.
- Towels, hand towels and pillows.
- Whatever products you use, such as massage oils, crystals or pendulums.
- An MP3 music player, candles, incense and sage smudges.

## *Business Items*

- Business cards and leaflets.
- A computer, tablet, or mobile phone.
- Telephone answering system or extra mobile phone.
- A ton of office odds and ends, including a stapler, paperclips, calculator, etc.
- A diary and address book.
- A picture frame in which to display a certificate if you have one.
- Books on your subject and other MBS subjects.
- Bookkeeping notebook or a laptop with spreadsheet or bookkeeping software.

## *Teaching*

- A whiteboard and flip charts, whiteboard markers and a cloth.
- Photocopied material to hand out.
- An extension cable and perhaps an extra light.
- Music or audio information on an MP3 player.
- A laptop, projector and screen for PowerPoint presentations.
- Transport.
- Business cards and leaflets.

# 6: Location and Family

If you have to work from home - especially after the Covid Pandemic - you may be able to rearrange your work to minimise the effect on family life. This may mean that you work while the family is sitting in front of the television, but that may be a small sacrifice to make, and these days there are many ways of catching up with a missed programme. If your family wants your company during the weekends, confine your work to weekdays, possibly working one or two evenings during the week to accommodate clients who can't come during the day. If your children are young, you may work during term times and stop during the school holidays. Trial and error will show you what works best for you and your family.

Some partners don't mind their loved one trotting off to psychic festivals, and they are sanguine about the partner staying away from home for a couple of nights now and then. However, others don't like it at all and don't want to accompany their partner. Festivals are usually run over weekends, so if your spouse wants your company at weekends, this may cause friction. If your partner is generally happy with your work but unhappy with the arrangements, you must devise a compromise.

Use a separate mobile phone for your work and leave the other phone(s) to the family for their calls, broadband, etc.

## *Spiritual Incompatibility*
Generally speaking, if a man is interested in astrology, rune reading, healing, herbalism or whatever, and if he lives with a woman, she will also take an interest in it. The aggravation usually occurs when the woman leads a spiritual life and the man does not. Some men find what we do weird, embarrassing or even frightening. They aren't interested in the subject and don't want to hear about it – or maybe they dislike seeing their partner doing

something they can't do themselves, and hate that others find their partner interesting in ways that they themselves are not.

Your relationship may be more important to you than your work, which may put the lid on your consultancy. However, if one person insists on having their way to the detriment of the other, this must be addressed. Occasional references to broomsticks can be fun, but frequent nasty remarks about your work or your beliefs are another matter.

One case I will never forget is of a man called John who came across a book on the tarot and taught himself to read the cards, discovering his psychic gifts as he went along. However, he dived pell-mell into the weirdest aspects of the paranormal, taking it to insane lengths because this gave him an outlet for his strange and intense personality. John's wife and children were interested in horses and spent most of their time at the stables, so needless to say, the wife and children soon rode off in one direction and John in another. The message here is that if your relationship is already in trouble, going pell-mell into spirituality, crystals, angels, reflexology or whatever might propel it to a swift conclusion.

* * *

Never drag a reluctant partner into your interests. Naturally, it would help if you answered any questions your partner comes up with but leave it at that. Don't push your ideas onto others, however deeply you believe in them yourself. Some people discover the alternative world and decide to dislike conventional doctors, hospitals and medicines. On the other hand, your partner may not wish to drink grey-green gunk instead of antibiotics when he is sick with a chest infection. The worst offenders are those new to our business. Remember, there is more to life. Do lots of other things and create a balance in your life.

The good news is that many happy relationships have been formed by people who meet through our kind of work. Some relationships turn into conventional life-long marriages while others are short-term affairs, but all are good in their own way.

### Female Consultants

The chances are that a male client has nothing further on his mind than having a reading or a therapy treatment, but you can't be sure, so think before you allow any old Tom, Dick and Harry into your abode. If you have a partner or older children, you could arrange to see your male clients when your loved ones are around. If you work some of the time with people everywhere, you can direct your male clients there and ensure that there are people in the building to call on in an emergency. Otherwise, you may seriously consider whether you want to deal with men at all.

Men can become highly agitated if they are going through a difficult time, and if a reading brings unpleasant feelings to the fore, they can become quite frightening. I have had angry men try to give me the same treatment they gave their wives, and I had to remind them that I was not their spouse, and I wasn't obliged to put up with nasty remarks, while being assaulted would end up with them serving a jail sentence.

One old boy who came to me for tarot readings on a fairly regular basis admitted that he liked dressing up in women's clothes. This didn't worry me because he really was a soft old duck, but it shows that you never know what's in the minds of your clients.

## *Male Consultants*

You can have as many problems with female clients as women have with males, but it works differently. Here is a true story about a good friend of mine.

George used to give healing at a healing centre now and again. He never took liberties with women, and he always worked when there were other healers around, but a woman decided to try and sue him for groping or something, and he had to call in a solicitor to help. She didn't get anywhere with her case because it was easy to prove that she was lying, but if people can try this on with George, they can do it to you.

It's a challenging world out there, so never say or do anything remotely flirtatious or unprofessional because even a mild joke can be taken the wrong way. If your client starts talking in a way that makes you uncomfortable, close the session immediately and refer her to a female consultant. If your client is pretty and you fancy her, keep it to yourself. Refer the client to someone else and do something more interesting with your time than sitting around and yearning. There are plenty of fish out there, so take a nice sea cruise and find a girlfriend for yourself.

Stay safe, be insured, and don't open yourself to trouble.

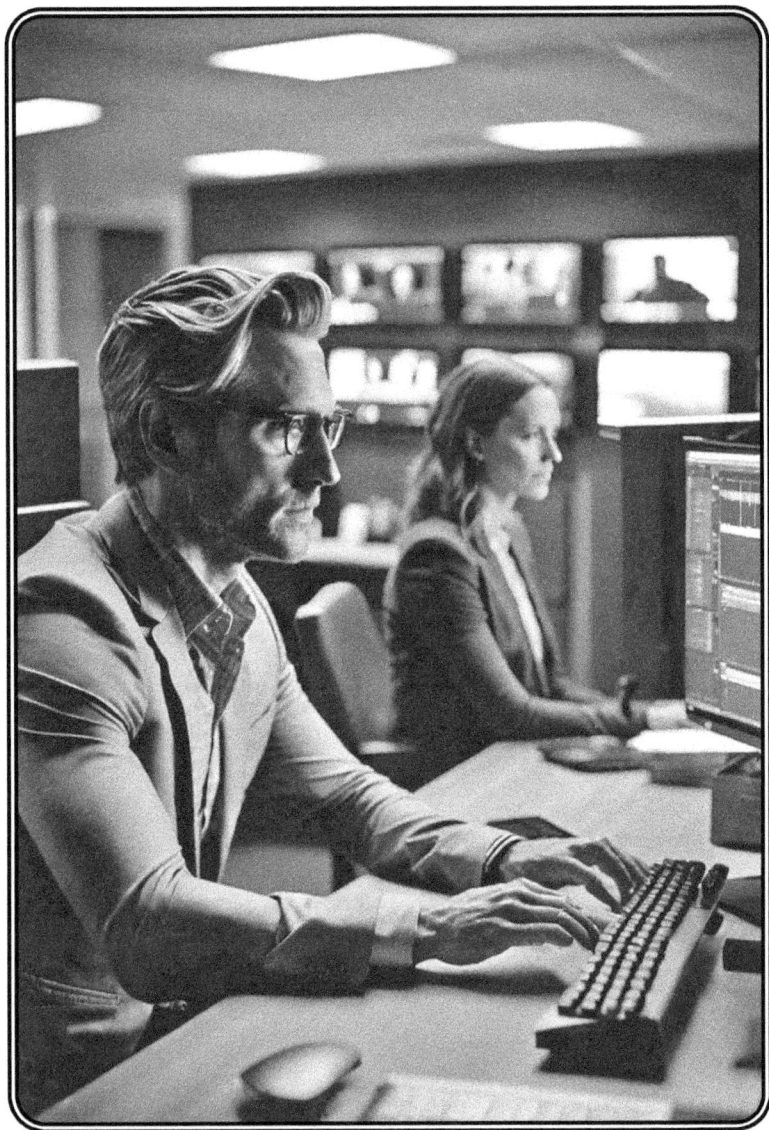

# 7: Financial Management

*"Annual income twenty pounds, annual expenditure nineteen
six, result happiness.
Annual income twenty pounds, annual expenditure twenty
pounds ought and six, result misery."*
DAVID COPPERFIELD (PUBLISHED IN 1850), BY CHARLES DICKENS.

The world of a Reader is not unlike that of an artist or actor, and
creative folk aren't necessarily good at the business side of things,
but we are in business, and it is better to acknowledge the fact and
take control of the situation. The first thing to consider is your
lifestyle, and it would be worth looking at the following list of
questions to see what you want to do. If your lifestyle changes in
the future, you can always re-read this section and see what
adjustments you need to make.

- Do you have a full or part-time job in addition to your
  consultancy?
- Are you retired or living on a pension?
- Are you home-based and receiving housekeeping money
  from a partner?
- Are you a full-time consultant with no other form of income?
- Are you disabled? Can you work in addition to receiving
  disablement benefits?
- What level of income do you need from your consultancy?

## Legitimate or Not Legitimate
Suppose you are only doing the occasional reading for people you
know personally. In that case, the payments you receive will be
cash and of no real importance, but you must be aware that even
this level of undeclared earnings can get you into hot water. When

you become truly professional or start dealing with the general public, you must put the business on a professional footing for your own sake.

During my time as a full-time professional Reader, an envelope from the Department of Social Security would plop through my letter box about three times a year. This would contain a small form asking for my National Insurance Number (Social Security Number). When I stopped being a Reader and seeing clients, I never received another of these forms, which confirmed my conclusion that once in a while, one of my clients would deliberately or inadvertently mention what I was doing to the Department of Social Security. I have no idea who "shopped" me on any of these occasions. Fortunately, my work was always legitimate, so when these forms arrived, I was happy to fill in my National Insurance number and give the DSS the name and address of my accountant. They never contacted my accountant, though.

## *A Bank Account*

You should open a separate bank account for your business as soon as your income goes beyond the level of an occasional bit of pocket money. If you have another full or part-time job or your partner gives you housekeeping money, you need to know whether you can budget on that alone or are beginning to rely on your Consultancy income. If your Readings are your primary source of income, you need to know precisely what is coming in from them and what is being spent. The second reason for a separate account is for tax purposes so that you can see your profit and work out (or ask your accountant to work out) your tax liability. Anybody in business for themselves needs to put aside a percentage of their income throughout the year for tax purposes and keep it separate from their other monies.

Shop around because banks offer many different kinds of services. Some banks offer a small overdraft facility free of charge and current accounts that pay interest. You may want to open a deposit (savings) account in addition to a current personal one to tuck away the money you will need for tax and other matters. Banks worldwide give out literature on their services, so look it all up on the internet and see what may be helpful to you.

If you already have a bank account, you may wish to stay with the same bank because it will be easier to move money from one account to another when needed. You may want to have accounts at different kinds of financial institutions, so look up all the schemes and see what will suit you best.

## *Benefits*

Depending upon your country and circumstances, you may receive some benefits, such as an old-age or disablement pension or a form of family credit or income support. The rules and regulations of what you can and cannot earn differ in every case, and you will need to look into these to establish your particular position. There may be a level of income or a number of working hours that you should not exceed, or it may not be tax efficient for you to earn over a certain amount. We cannot give specific advice in this book, but we suggest you survey your position and make the most effective decisions. You may need to talk to an accountant.

## *Budgeting and Saving*

Whatever your lifestyle, it is worth working out a weekly or monthly budget to know how much you need to live on. If you are earning enough to live on and have something left over, put ten per cent of your net income away for the future, perhaps by setting up a scheme that allows you to save monthly.

## *Cashflow*

Cashflow means having enough money behind you to carry you through times when income is slow. Most businesses have slow times, often at specific times of the year, but as long as a business owner has money put by, the lean period is easy to ride out. You need to keep some money in hand to cover slow times; or a separate job that pays the main bills.

Your clientele will slow right down or even dry up entirely from around the last week in November while people prepare for Christmas. Another slow time in the UK occurs in June, just before the family holiday season. A good time starts at the latter stage of the main holiday season, possibly because relationships are often under strain at this time. Therapists dealing with physical pain might also be busy at that time, and people often put their backs out when carting baggage about or when sleeping in uncomfortable beds. Tummy upsets and sunburn might also need treatment after a holiday.

## *No Real Reason*

Sometimes there are weeks when the phone doesn't ring or when several clients fail to turn up. You may be charging too much, so it might be worth dropping your prices for a while and seeing whether that helps. A less obvious reason is that your spiritual guides may decide you need a break. While this is irritating, all you can do is go with the flow and enjoy the time off. If business remains slow after a couple of weeks, review everything you are doing to see if you can think of anything to improve matters.

It is just possible that you are being blocked, either by a jealous person or a spiritual entity. In a typical business situation, such a suggestion would sound absolutely crazy, but we know that such things are possible. Try the following ideas:

- Bless the business. Bless the door to the premises, the premises themselves, the tools you use, your suppliers, your clients and everything else you can think of.
- Treat yourself to a book on Feng Shui and do what you can to improve the energy flow around your place of work.
- If you think someone is blocking your progress, do a meditation that involves surrounding yourself with mirrors that let in good vibes while keeping bad ones out.
- Make a talisman, buy a lucky charm, and meditate upon it to bring business your way.
- Buy green, red and orange crystals, and prepare them by washing in spring water and passing them through the smoke of an incense stick, and then keep them close to where you work.

## *Don't Give Up Your Day Job*

If you have a job you can tolerate and that brings in money, you should keep it. Depending on your circumstances, you may get to a stage where you can give it up for good. You can afford to concentrate all your energies on your consultancy if you have some other form of income, but if you don't, you may have to accept that your business will never reach a point where it keeps you.

Whatever happens in life, you must also keep up National Insurance payments and fill in any gaps if you haven't paid the full amount. Never pay the reduced rate for low earners because this will prevent you from getting a full state pension later. If your "proper job" carries a good pension scheme or other perks, you would be silly to throw these away.

Consultancy work isn't reliable, and there are times of the year when it disappears off the face of the earth, so having another job to turn to may well be essential. If you do make consulting the centre of your working life, other jobs can provide a welcome change of pace, and they can fill in the gaps when your regular business is slow.

There is no need to make a lifetime commitment to working as a consultant. You may spend several years doing a day job and giving healing or readings on the side, and then perhaps go into consulting full-time. You may concentrate on something entirely different for a few years and return to your consultancy later on a part-time basis once again. You may combine readings or treatments with something artistic or creative. A part-time hairdresser who gives readings and cares for her young family is a good example.

| QUANTITY | ITEM | AMOUNT £ |
|---|---|---|
| 1 | READING | 60.00 |
| 3 OR MORE | READINGS | 150.00 |
| EVENING GROUP | MULTIPLE SHORT READINGS, EACH | 40.00 |
| DAY GROUPS | MULTIPLE SHORT READINGS, EACH | 40.00 |
| 10 | PSYCHIC FAIR — 10 READINGS AT £25 EACH | 250.00 |

# 8: Charges and Fees

Most consultants charge far too little, especially if they lack confidence or fear they won't get any work if they charge a higher fee. Consultants just starting out may feel that they aren't ready to charge much, which is fair enough, but consultants should increase their prices when they gain confidence.

Working in a high-income area is possible, even if you can't afford to live in one, as long as you are prepared to travel and rent premises. The rental may be expensive, but it might include reception and booking facilities, and as long as there are plenty of well-heeled clients, the cost will be worthwhile. Otherwise, you could consider the following ideas, which Sasha gathered together from several other Consultants:

- See what others who do similar work charge.
- Check the cost of going to a hairdresser for a cut, colour and blow-dry, including the tip and charge about the same. If you're a man, ask a typical hairdresser about their prices.
- Consider what you would expect to earn in a regular job, and break down the monthly or annual salary into hourly rates. You will probably consider the rate low, but employees are paid whether they are fully occupied or not.

## *Hidden Costs*

Remember that the money you earn from your readings is not free and clear. You may have to pay income tax and National Insurance (Social Security), and you will pay something for the space you use, the equipment you need, the phone, transport and marketing. There are always hidden expenses that can take you by surprise, and even such things as water, tea, coffee and loo rolls must be paid for.Keep receipts for everything you use, as it can all be put against income tax.

## *Facts and Fantasies*

There are always stories about people who charge massive fees and apparently get away with this. Ignore these tales because they are unlikely to be true.

Some clients will expect you to charge what they paid way back in the past.

Some clients will expect your services to be free, either because it is well-known that your talent comes from God and should therefore have to be given away free of charge or because the client is confusing your therapeutic consultancy with the National Health Service.

Some will phone up and try to get you to drop your price for them because they are old, disabled, out of work or out of luck.

## *Time is Money*

When making the appointment, tell the client what you charge. If the client dumps you at this point, so be it. If they want the services for far less than you charge, thank them for enquiring and tell them you can't accept them as clients.

Group your clients together so you work on specific days or times. If you have a string of clients, the only one who can try to outstay his time is the last one.

After a particularly helpful reading, some clients will offer you more than you have quoted; take this, as this is the client's way of thanking you. Similarly, if a regular client brings you flowers or a little present, accept this gracefully; it is lovely when this happens.

Always give good value for money. You don't need to sort out every area of a client's life, but you must do your job as well as you can.

Don't fall into the trap of thinking that someone who works across town is better at the job than you are. We all work differently, and your method may differ from theirs.

## *When Things Go Wrong*

Only take money from the client when you have finished the job, unless it's a remote session. If a client gives you the money before you start, leave it lying openly on your table and only pick it up and put it away when the work is done. If the work goes wrong for some reason, do not charge the client. Usher them off the premises quickly and write the situation down to experience.

## *Perception*

We sometimes hear comments about charlatans, but when we ask the person to name the charlatan, nothing emerges. The problem can be perception because some clients want more than anyone can be expected to give, or they may want a different kind of service from the one on offer. An example may be a client who goes to a palmist or an astrologer who tells them about their future trends when they really need a medium to get through to their late Aunty Fanny. A crystal therapist is not a reflexologist, and a Reiki healer is not a masseur. I'm sure you get the idea. Some want to hear specific news, such as being assured of winning a large lottery sum or finding a rich husband, and they get miffed if you can't guarantee this for them.

Some consultants plunge into business before they have enough skill or experience, and these should only charge a small fee until they get on top of the job.

Everybody has days they are ill, worried or just not in the mood for the demands of clients. If you find yourself in a phase like this, cancel your clients for a while and reschedule them for later.

Some consultants become stale but can't stop because they need the money. They really should stop for a while, do something else to bring in money and come back to consulting after a break when they feel good about it again.

## *Freeloaders*

One irritating form of freeloading is the person who phones you and asks you to tell them "just one little thing" about flower essences, astrology or whatever it is you do. They then expect you to spend the rest of the day giving them a free tutorial or a full intunement, induction or whatever. Suggest they look online for answers. You may feel that you are turning a potential client away, but these people aren't ever going to become clients, only nuisances.

## *Fraudulent Mediums*

The old days of fraudulent mediums with a whole baggage of tricks to make their clients believe that ghosts and spirits were moaning, wailing and levitating stuff around their rooms have gone. These days, the public is far too well informed to believe such old hocus-pocus.

That said, there are still chancers who will try to defraud their clients, and that is a very good reason for you to have a qualification and certificate as proof that you are the real thing.

## *Disclaimers*

If you need a disclaimer, have it typed up, frame it and put it on your desk or your wall in clear view and remind any clients who become difficult of its contents. I should add here that in the UK, current legislation is such that most Readers do need a disclaimer. Investigate what wording is best for your particular work and use it.

# 9: Bookkeeping and the Tax Man

Bookkeeping can be simple or comprehensive depending on the scale of your operations, but the primary need is to record what comes in and what goes out. You can call this income and expenses, purchases and sales, or whatever you like. The simplest method is to buy two notebooks, one for your income and one for expenses. Starting with your expenses, your first step is to draw three columns and note the date, supplier and the goods, and amount. Above all, keep all the receipts for your purchases, and keep them in the order they appear in your notebook. If the receipts are small, staple them to larger pieces of paper and file the lot in a lever-arch file.

| DATE 2023 | SUPPLIER AND GOODS | AMOUNT £ |
|---|---|---|
| 25 JAN | PC WORLD, PRINTER | 150.00 |
| 27 JAN | RYMANS, STATIONERY ITEMS | 14.00 |
| 31 JAN | ASDA, TOP-UP FOR MOBILE | 10.00 |
| 5 FEB | ADVANCE FEE: MAY-DAY PSYCHIC FAIR | 50.00 |

Whether your consultancy is your only job or you have a day job elsewhere, you will find that you can put an amazing number of expenses against your tax bill, to the point where you will end up paying very little Income Tax, if any at all. It is no good telling your accountant or the tax man that you spent money on such and such an item unless you can prove it, so right from day one, keep all receipts!

### *How Long Do You Need to Keep Records?*

Legally you need to keep your records for six years, but it is probably best to keep them for at least ten. You can buy archive boxes at any stationer, put the old records in these and shove them in the loft, but don't forget to get them down again when you move house.

### *Keeping Your Diary Records*

If you ever have the bad luck of being investigated by the tax department, they will want to see your appointment diaries so they can match the number of clients you have seen to the amount of money you have declared. Such logs must be kept for six years along with your books. If you are not in the habit of declaring the full amount of your income in your books, your diaries will catch you. Many pop singers, film stars and successful artists have been caught out this way. If a large tax bill does come, it won't happen when times are good, but long after the gravy train has gone; it will be hard to find the money.

### *Sample Record of Your Income*

Keep everything related to the bigger forms of income, such as details of the psychic fairs and the enquiry about the woman's magazine article. The smaller items will be in your diary.

| DATE 2023 | SOURCE OF INCOME | AMOUNT £ |
|---|---|---|
| 1 JAN | READING | 60.00 |
| 7 JAN | TALK AT A LOCAL CLUB | 25.00 |
| 10 JAN | READING | 60.00 |
| 30 JAN | ARTICLE FOR SPECIAL WOMAN MAGAZINE | 25.00 |
| 4 FEB | PSYCHIC FAIR – 10 READINGS AT £25 EACH | 250.00 |

## Spreadsheets

If you like spreadsheets, the next table shows how you can separate items. The amounts in the Totals columns and rows should add up to the same figure, which becomes your checksum.

| DATE | SUPPLIER | TRANSPORT | STATIONERY | PHONE/POST | TOTALS |
|---|---|---|---|---|---|
| 4 JAN | GARAGE | 70.00 | | | 70.00 |
| 7 JAN | WH SMITH | | 12.00 | | 12.00 |
| 10 JAN | BT | | | 95.00 | 95.00 |
| 14 JAN | POSTAGE | | | 7.00 | 7.00 |
| TOTALS FOR | JANUARY | 70.00 | 12.00 | 102.00 | 184.00 |

## Spreadsheet Tips

Any form of record keeping will show you at a glance what you are spending and cut down your accountancy bill. Set aside a particular time - say once a fortnight and do it religiously.

If your income and outgoings are not great, a simple list of incoming and outgoing monies on paper will be enough, but if your business takes off, you will need a bookkeeping system. There are plenty on the market, but perhaps a simple form of QuickBooks would be the best. If you are very good at techie things, you can even do your books on your mobile, but take care that it doesn't get lost or stolen.

## Do You Need an Accountant?

You will need help with tax forms, and you will need to be able to prove to the Department of Work and Pensions that you are not working in the black economy. If you try to work without declaring your income, it will be no more than three months before someone shops you.

## *Can You Have a Job and Also Run a Business?*
### *Yes, but speak to your accountant about it.*

The two organisations that you really shouldn't try to fool are the Department of Work and Pensions (DWP) and the VAT man. If you are working in Britain, as soon as you are up and running, you must apply to the DWP to pay your National Insurance contributions. There are different contribution levels, and if you earn very little, your contribution can be reduced or even temporarily set aside, but this will affect your pension, so it is worth stumping up the full amount. If you are not in the UK, you will need advice on your local situation.

As a self-employed consultant in the UK, you will find that you can roll losses or your start-up expenditure forward for several years, which will reduce your tax bill when things take off. Once again, check your local situation.

VAT (Value Added Tax) only applies to larger businesses, so you won't qualify for this. You will pay VAT on the things you buy, though, just as we all do when shopping.

### *Don't Fiddle*
If yours is a cash business, it is easy to slip money into your own pocket without declaring it, but there are drawbacks. For instance, you may want to ask your bank for a loan, and if you haven't shown a reasonable income on your books, how is the bank supposed to believe that you will be able to pay them back? In such a case, they will refuse the loan.

Keep good records, pay your National Insurance and Income Tax and sleep well at night.

### *Avoidance of Unnecessary Taxation*
If you are into meditating or chanting, you will find this exercise easy; if you are not, then try this. Visualise a nasty, complicated tax form while you relax in a scented bath and recite to yourself twenty times over...

"Keep all receipts, keep all receipts, keep all receipts, keep all receipts..."

This kind of transcendental meditation will lower your blood pressure, slow your heart rate, keep lines off your face, keep the hair on your head and improve a saggy bottom. In addition to all this, it will save you a fortune!

Do your bookkeeping because the number of things you can put against tax is incredible, and you can save a fortune by being canny with your purchases and receipts. Frankly, anything that can even vaguely be deemed a business expense will work, and the following list of ideas may help you to see where tax savings can be made. If you do make an invalid claim, your accountant will spot it and leave it out of the equation.

### *Tax Deductible Expenses*

The following list covers several expenses that, to our best knowledge, are currently deductible for a self-employed person. The regulations change from time to time, so always check the latest information.

Travel by public transport. Keep all tickets, including bus tickets! If your train tickets disappear into an automatic machine, keep a vague note of how much you spend per week on train travel. Ask taxi drivers for a receipt.

- Hotel bills.
- Insurance.
- Membership of relevant organisations.
- Stationery items, office paraphernalia and all such bits and pieces.
- Books of any kind, even those unrelated to your work. Who can say what books you may need to read for research purposes?
- Magazines and papers.
- Your computer, tablet and office machinery.
- Office services – such as getting things laminated.
- Phones and phone bills of all kinds.
- Recording equipment.

If you broadcast, you can put part of the cost of your own television, radio and video against tax. Small radios may be wholly deductible. In the UK, you can even put the cost of your TV licence against tax if you are an occasional TV performer. It is unlikely that the tax man would require proof of this but keep a video of any programme that you appear on as proof.

- Dry cleaning and ironing (small amounts would be acceptable).
- Anything you pay others to do for you in connection with your work. If you farm jobs out to others, get them to give you a signed note showing their charges.
- Coffee, tea, milk, biscuits, loo rolls, and some cleaning costs that result from you having people in for readings.
- Tarot cards, crystal balls, dowsing rods and anything else to do with your work.
- A course of training related to your work.
- A consultation with a guru? Ask your accountant about this one!
- Your vehicle.

Interestingly, you can put a car and all expenses that go with it against income tax. This is not the case for a Limited Company, though, unless the vehicle is a van specifically used for the business. Don't forget to keep your petrol receipts and any servicing receipts.

### Some Viable Expenses

If you work from home, you can offset a small amount against your tax bill to cover a proportion of your household costs. Your accountant will advise you on this. The amount is not large, but every little helps. This situation applies whether you rent or own your own home. Do take some advice on the situation regarding Capital Gains Tax because if you claim tax relief against your mortgage over the years, you may have to pay some of this back later.

Subsistence is a fancy word for food and drink, and you can set this against tax if you travel on business. One Reader told us she always chooses hotels that provide breakfast, as that comes under deductible expenses. Travel expenses should be deductible as long as you can show they are for business.

You may not be able to claim the full cost of buying and running a vehicle against tax, but you should be able to claim part of it. You may have difficulty claiming the whole of your telephone or mobile phone bill, but you might be able to claim some of it. Ask your accountant.

You can put a certain amount of expense against tax without producing receipts. You can't be too fanciful, but a reasonable-sounding amount is acceptable.

In the UK, the only trades or professions that allow tax relief on clothing are those where it can be proved that the clothes can never be used for anything other than work, including therapy outfits and the linens used in the therapy room. You can claim for dry cleaning for your ordinary clothes, for taking towels and linens to the laundrette, or for the washing capsules you buy.

### *Don't be Afraid to Communicate*
Tax and other officials are approachable and helpful, and if you don't have an accountant, they will help you fill in your self-assessment forms and advise you on what you can claim. Having said this, the chances are that all communication will be online now, rather than the phone.

### *A Final Word*
Whatever you do, please don't allow a situation to drift along without dealing with it. Be honest. Declare your earnings and pay your way. Your tax bill won't amount to much anyway – if anything at all - and self-employment is hard enough without worrying about tax irregularities.

Always ensure that your claims and expenses are correct and that you understand the law as it applies to your line of work. It's true that "ignorance of the law is no excuse."

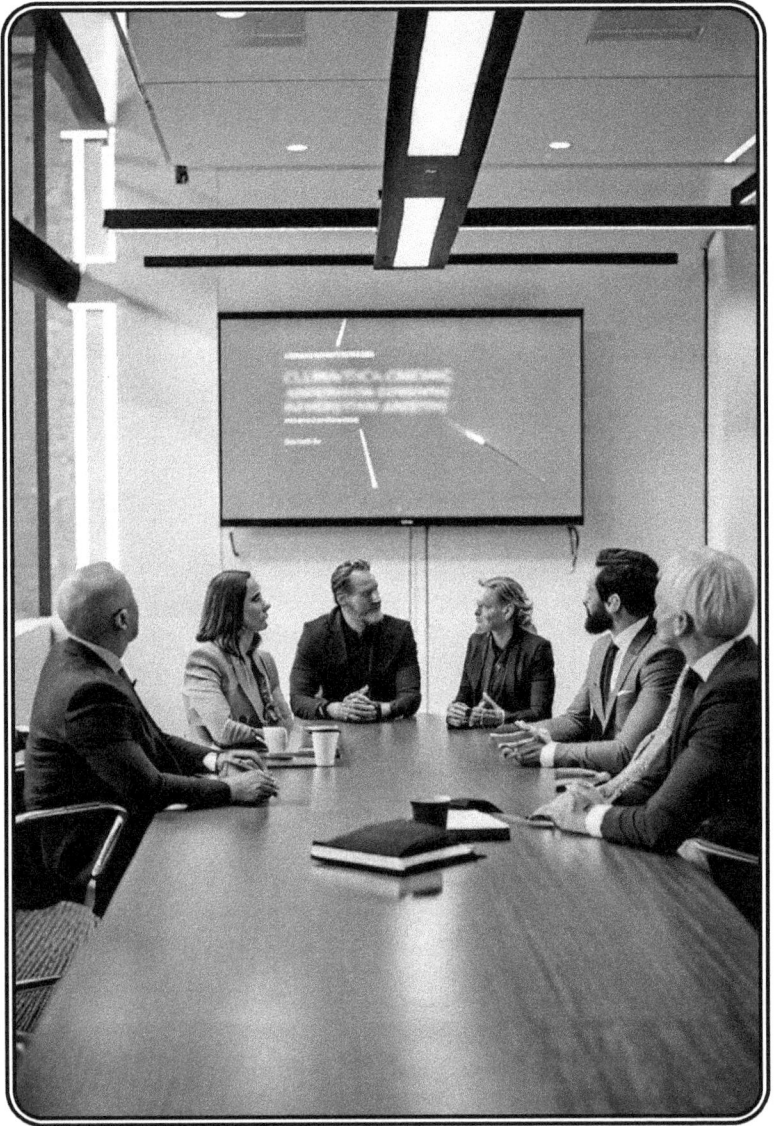

# 10: Organisational Methods

Jan once watched a television programme about the paranormal, and we were interested to note that one of the mediums who travelled out to his clients and his talks and demonstrations, had all the arrangements made by his brother. The chances are that when you are just starting, you will have to do these things yourself, but this shouldn't be too difficult.

## *Appointments*
Like any other businessperson, you will need a diary which may be paper or a calendar on your phone or tablet. If there is the slightest chance that the tax man will likely investigate you, use a paper diary and keep your diaries for at least six years. Diaries can sometimes be useful when you need to find a name, a phone number or an address. If you jot down a client's phone number against their name when they make an appointment, then you have it handy if you need to change the appointment date or time.

## *The Telephone*
This is one of the best inventions of the 20th century (in my opinion, it ranks alongside the washing machine as a mark of true human progress,) but the telephone can also be a tyrant. In the days before answering machines, consultants had to take calls day and night whether they wanted to or not. You might find it helpful to have a different phone for family and friends to the one you use for business, and you can turn the business phone off when you have finished work.

## *Technology*
If you give lessons or lectures, have to write letters or create invoices, you will need something to type on and a printer to print

your documents. If you are an astrologer, you will definitely need to use a computer or tablet and software for your charts.

### Letterhead, Leaflets and Business Cards

The last thing you need is to buy a heap of expensively printed letterhead for your business, but you might want to get some leaflets printed to show what you do, and business cards can be a good investment.

### Time Management

Have an admin blitz every couple of days. Open your post, deal with paperwork, appointments and bills, file things and get them out of the way. If you pile stuff into a tray and leave it, you will only have to plough through it again later and lose track of important bits of paper.

Elect specific days and times for seeing clients and stick to them. Elect days for family stuff, housework, working on the car, visiting friends and so on - and stick to them.

Make batch bookings for your clients so you don't break up the flow of your day. (More about this below...)

The third item in this list of tips is worth a little thought. A client's visit to a consultant is an occasion, and they are happy to drag it out. For many, this is probably the only time in their lives that someone concentrates exclusively on them and wants to help them, but inexperienced Readers or therapists can end up with a client who takes up a whole afternoon or evening. You can avoid this problem by booking several clients at suitable intervals during the day or the evening. Work out how long each reading should take and add fifteen minutes to each appointment. If you only have one reading booked for a day or your last client looks set to stay on, you just have to tell them their time is up. A consultant once told me she lights a candle at the start of each session, and she stands up and blows it out when she feels the session is at an end. A clock is invaluable in being able to time your sessions.

### Visiting Clients

Unless you are going out to give a talk or for a party-plan session, only visit clients in their own homes if you know them well, if you really need to do so, or if you have a great urge to be a social worker. Ensure that someone - usually your partner - knows the address where you are going and when you should be back. The time and money you spend on travelling, finding the infernal place and finding parking is only part of the problem; the chances are that your client just wants company. Lonely people will ply you with tea and homemade cakes and show you photographs of their grandchildren, and while this is all very well, is it practical on a business basis? I am also wary of suggesting that you go unaccompanied into a stranger's home, because you can't be sure of your safety. Don't take chances with strangers or even people you've met a few times.

## *Sasha's Story*

Even a foolhardy activity can have educational value. I remember visiting a client who said that she had no way of coming to see me. When I arrived, I found a gentle, slim, beautiful young woman whose clothes were far more fashionable and expensive than anything I could afford. She appeared to spend her days sitting in a lovely apartment and doing nothing other than watching television. Her reading revealed a life that was utterly empty but extremely comfortable, but after I had gone through the main points of what I could find in her Tarot card reading, her conversation became very strange. She seemed to be quietly and gently crazy as she went on about how tigers came through the walls at her and much else of the same ilk. It transpired that she lived with a minor rock star, and her fragile mental state was probably due to drug-taking.

At the time, my lifestyle was the polar opposite of her existence as a beautiful, pampered "lily of the field", but after some thought, I realised that nothing would induce me to exchange my lifestyle for hers!

## *Allied Work*

You might give talks about what you do or even manage to get a part-time job with a local authority, as some run classes on aromatherapy, Reiki and so on. You will need to look into the tax implications, but even that isn't a real problem.

# 11: Building a Clientele

*'If you have something you wish to sell, don't go whispering it down a well.'*
AMERICAN PROVERB

## *Advertising in Papers and Magazines*

Many years ago, I advertised my services in a local newspaper, but all it brought was heavy breathers. I found it better to advertise in a mind, body and spirit magazine or perhaps a woman's magazine. You will be in competition with many others that way, but they don't all live in your area, and clients are usually looking for consultants who work in their own location. Look at the other advertisements and copy the style of those that catch your eye. A photograph is always eye-catching.

## *Word of Mouth*

If you are starting out, give friends free consultations and business cards to pass on to their friends and colleagues. It might even be worth trawling through your phone list and contacting everyone you know to suggest they visit you or have a telephone consultation. In short, anything that gets the ball rolling will help.

## *Business Cards and Leaflets*

Always give a client two business cards, one for the client and one to pass on to a friend. Always carry a few business cards with you. Bless your business cards, brochures and other marketing material and tell clients they will bring them good luck. They probably will if blessed, so this isn't a lie.

You don't need to spend a fortune on business cards because there are companies who print nice ones really cheaply. Get help designing a logo and with the techie side of emailing the material to the printer.

Don't order a large number of cards or literature because you may decide you want to change them, but once you know you are on the right track, you can get larger quantities printed.

Nowadays, people don't always put their addresses on their material, so you must decide what you want to advertise and what you want to keep private. A website would be helpful; at the very least, you need an email address.

### *Other Forms of Advertising*

- Your local clinic may be happy to put a card on their notice board for you.
- Try your local gym or tennis club, especially if you offer therapies.
- If you know any students, ask them to put a notice on their college board.
- Ask friends who work in large firms if they can put your leaflet on the notice board.
- If you specialise in horoscopes for children and babies, ask your local mother and baby shop to display a holder full of your leaflets.
- Employ a couple of youngsters to hand out your leaflets to shoppers outside a supermarket.

You can slip leaflets into doorways, and if your feet give out, you can pay local schoolchildren to do this for you. Mail-order specialists will tell you that you can expect about a two to four per cent take-up on leaflets, so bear in mind that on this basis, 200 leaflets will bring you four to eight clients. If you do try this route, keep your leaflets small and inexpensive.

### *Talks, Lectures and Demonstrations*

Contact your local mother's group, wine appreciation society, garden club, Masonic Ladies, Rotarians and any other group that uses speakers. You don't have to confine yourself to women's groups, but you are more likely to get spin-off business from women than from men. You can locate such groups by asking your friends and colleagues, visiting your local library or looking online. Ensure everyone has a leaflet to take away with them.

You won't receive much money from any of these activities, but you will meet friendly people, and as long as you hand out your leaflets or business cards, you should get some business later. If there are any self-development or self-awareness groups in your area, offer to give them a talk. If you are in the Spiritualist movement, you can give readings or counselling sessions for charity. Charity organisations may be happy to use you; sometimes, even a local firm will book you as an after-dinner speaker. Some of these events pay a fee; some only pay travel expenses, and some won't pay anything at all, but they are all worth doing. Remember to put leaflets and cards on all the chairs so everyone gets them.

Organisations book their speakers several months ahead, so diarise everything in advance. Also, keep any letters and other information in a file so you can put your hands on them when needed. Keep any contact details and perhaps a map or instructions about finding the venue.

Keep things very simple if speaking to a group not into your subject. Involving the audience by giving them a chance to dowse with rods or pendulums or giving some sample tarot readings that everyone can listen to or handing round crystals for people to hold or anything else of the kind always goes down well.

If you give a talk to a group well into your subject, ask the organisers about the standard of your audience and pitch your lecture accordingly. If your audience is of a high level, pitch your talk to that level. If you think you are likely to do more than the occasional talk, treat yourself to a cardboard, table-based flip chart with tear-off sheets of paper. This is cheaper to buy and easier to cart about than a heavy whiteboard. If the venue has a whiteboard, don't expect them to have any whiteboard markers or cleaning cloth - take your own along.

The venue's whiteboard may be covered in permanent marking that won't brush off with a cloth, but nail-polish remover will get it off, so buy some and take it with you.

If you are using PowerPoint for an important event, don't depend upon the venue to have a laptop or a projector; even if they insist that they do, take your own. Even buy a small screen on eBay and bring that along as well.

Jan and I once did an important event where we invited several authors to discuss their work while we showed a PowerPoint presentation about their books. The talk was in a brand, spanking new library, and the organisers told us that all we needed to bring along was a memory stick with our authors' material on it. When we arrived, we found that the connection point for the projector had been smashed to smithereens earlier that day by someone who had tried to squeeze the wrong kind of plug into it, and the venue's laptop had vanished. Fortunately, we had brought our own gear along, so although it was a pain to set up, we delivered the material as scheduled.

## The Media

Contact your local paper and see if they would like a feature on you. You could write a piece on what you do, how you got into the business and maybe even tell a couple of amusing stories about your experiences. You won't be paid, but if the paper prints your story, this will bring you to the public's attention. Instruct the newspaper to pass your phone number on to anybody who enquires after a reading. You can be sure that the people at the paper will want a free reading, therapy or Reiki session, or whatever you do.

Your local radio station may be persuaded to interview you, but you might be asked to talk to the public on a phone-in basis. Radio stations are besieged with people who want to be on their shows, and producers and presenters are wary of newcomers or unknowns, so you should leave this until you have a track record. If you do decide to become a radio star, maybe work up some divination that is a bit different from the norm, something like Feng Shui for cats, maybe!

## Too Many Clients

After a while, you may become saturated with clients. I can almost hear you saying that you'd welcome that problem. Believe me, it can happen, and it needs a bit of careful handling because while trying to see all those who contact you is tempting, you must avoid working yourself into the ground. Take breaks, get away from the job occasionally and enjoy your family.

## Nuisance Phone Callers

You will inevitably get the occasional heavy breather if you are a woman. If you have a man around, hand the phone over to him because as soon as the caller hears a man's voice, he will go away. This kind of caller doesn't want to deal with a woman who is "protected" by another male. Otherwise, turn the phone off.

Many years ago, before mobile phones existed, a poor Reader was plagued by dozens of calls that came at all hours of the day and night, and all she heard was a beeping sound. Even her answering machine didn't stop it, and she soon discovered that the caller was rewinding the tape on the device and listening to her messages. She put in a separate line for family and friends so she could keep that phone on and keep in touch with those who really needed to be able to contact her, and she fixed a removable phone jack onto the business line, which she disconnected at night. The problem soon went away.

Here is a true story. A tarot reading colleague started getting a series of frightening "heavy-breather" calls. She had recently taken up with a new man, and when she told him about the problem, he appeared to be very concerned and worried about it. One day when my colleague and I were discussing the problem, I had a sudden psychic flash telling me that it was the new boyfriend who was making the calls. My colleague didn't want to believe this, but when I asked her if the calls ever came in when her boyfriend was with her, she realised they did not. She called his bluff, and it turned out that my psychic flash was right; it was him! Needless to say, she promptly dumped him.

## Charity Events

Be very careful with any charity attached to a church or other religious institution, as the people there may not like what you do, especially if it involves the Tarot.

# 12: Skills and Qualifications

You don't need any special qualifications to become a Tarot reader or a medium, although you might wish to become accredited by an organisation such as MBS Professionals Ltd. However, anyone who treats the public, such as therapists, counsellors etc., must belong to professional organisations and be fully qualified and registered.

In the past, the European Union posed problems for herbalists and others of a similar ilk by trying to outlaw their work. However, we are no longer part of the EU, so these people only need any therapist's standard qualifications and accreditations.

## *Beginners*

If you are a beginner, you may feel unsure of your abilities, and if so, look around for skill-building opportunities. If you are over-confident, you will soon fall flat on your face - at which point you will either give up or decide that you could do with a bit more information and training. The best way to gain experience is to do the job, but you may have to work without charging a fee until you are comfortable with your skills.

Look online for training opportunities, join relevant organisations and sign their codes of ethics. Read magazines that specialise in your craft and go for a Reiki session, visit spiritualist churches to watch the mediums at work or have readings. Above all, buy books on your subject and read them.

Don't get hung up on one particular "guru" or influencer who you like but read widely and try out a variety of ideas. Filter all you hear through a layer of common sense.

### Groups

You may join a group or organisation only to find that the members are stand-offish, unfriendly and unwelcoming, but give it a bit of time because you may find others within the group who are pleasant and helpful. If this doesn't happen within a month or two, find another group with a better vibe.

Those who serve on committees of organisations should welcome new members and ask the older members to look after the newbies, but this rarely happens, and newcomers are often left floundering. If an organisation finds itself wringing its hands because they don't have enough members, or nobody wants to do any work for the organisation, they should check out their own behaviour and see what it is be like for strangers who come up against them.

### Sasha's Story

As a long-term diabetic who also has atrial fibrillation, the last thing my body needs is extra weight, so every now and then, I feel the need to lose a stone or so, and I take myself to a slimming club for a while. A few years ago, I went to a group that was new to me, and when I walked in, I saw the usual arrangement of two women sitting behind a table, one who books people in and takes their payments and another who weighs the people and notes down their weight-loss etc. I knew these women were volunteers, and volunteers don't get any training, so they may or may not be good at dealing with the public.

On this occasion, I walked up to the money lady, who told me in no uncertain terms that I was too early and should return later. Her attitude was so unwelcoming that I was on the point of walking out for good when the weighing-in lady jumped up and welcomed me, suggesting that I sit with some other ladies and chat for a few minutes while the money lady waited for the right time to open her computer and cash box. As it happened, I knew a bit about how the organisation worked, and I knew that the money lady couldn't open her computer system earlier than her set time because the system was hooked up to a network that prevented this. Still, being scowled at and told to go away wasn't nice.

As it happened, the group's location suited me, and I stayed for a few weeks and lost the weight I needed to lose. I became friendly with the lovely lady who had welcomed me, but I never bothered to speak to the other silly woman.

I had a similar experience in the early 1980s when I first joined the British Astrological and Psychic Society - with not one but two idiotic women who made me feel unwelcome. I didn't give up on the Society, though, as I needed their accreditation to work at festivals. As it happened, soon after I joined, both women left the committee, and I was invited to serve on it. I served as Secretary for several years, always welcoming new members and making them feel valued.

# 13: Fairs and Festivals

You may wish to work at various events, and the range is quite extensive, so let us start with the smallest and work our way up.

## *Local Fetes*

Your local school or hospital may put on a fete, and you may consider offering your services as a "fortune-teller" for the day. You will probably do this on a charitable basis, taking no money for yourself, but handing out business cards to those who consult you. This is a surprisingly effective way of drumming up future business.

Craft fairs, antique fairs, flea markets and so on can be worthwhile if the space you rent for the day is not too expensive. They don't generate much business, but it is still worth a try if the event is in your locality. If there is a regular local flea market in your area, it could be worth renting a table permanently as long as the event is indoors. A friend of mine says that these events are invaluable for beginners, as they force you to deal with the public rather than friends and family, which helps you build experience and confidence.

There may be regulations against people giving readings or other such services at local boot sales and the like, so check out the rules before visiting such venues. Such things as county fairs and horse fairs may be useful, but these can be the province of the Traveller community, which won't welcome competition. Always double-check with the authorities whenever possible.

## *Psychic Fairs and Festivals*

There are many psychic and mystic festivals around, varying greatly in size and scope. The success of these events depends upon the amount of local advertising that the organisers arrange and on unforeseen factors such as the weather and competing events. I remember one festival in Basildon that was a dead loss because it was held on the same day as a much more popular county fair. On the other hand, the day of the football Cup-Final is good because the men-folk are glued to the television, and many women are free to do what they want, including going for a nice massage or whatever.

If you decide to work at a psychic festival, find out the cost of renting space and the size of the allocated area. You can rent a single table, or you might wish to share one. Work out how far you will have to travel if you need to stay somewhere overnight, and whether that makes the event worth the cost and effort. Make a checklist of things you need to do and the things you need to take with you; keep it on file as a template for subsequent events, adding more items over time. Here are a few ideas:

- A vehicle to take yourself and all your baggage to the event. You might share a ride with someone else, thus helping to keep costs down.
- A small table in addition to the space that you rent. There isn't always space for this at small fairs, but there might be – in which case it's handy to have one on the car.
- Keep a comfortable folding chair in the car in case the ones supplied are "back-breakers". Also, a cushion to sit on.
- A collection of stationery items and a "Swiss Army penknife".
- Cards and pens on which you can write notices, prices, etc.
- An MP3 recorder/player, a lamp and adaptors, extension leads and tape for sticking wires to the floor.
- Cloths to spread on the table.
- A couple of flasks of hot water for tea and coffee. Also, tea, coffee, sugar, paper towels, travel wipes, a spoon, a knife, sandwiches, fruit, cans of soft drinks or bottled water.
- In cold weather, take a pre-filled hot water bottle, and top it up with more hot water at the venue.

### *Tools of your trade.*
- A float for change and a box to keep it in.

- Business cards and leaflets or brochures and display holders for them.
- Extra warm clothes. Most fairs are held in cold places, and if you happen to be by a door, you will freeze. Also, changes of clothes if the weather or conditions are changeable or if you intend to be away overnight.
- Pain killers, indigestion tablets, plasters and any particular medicines.
- An angel or Buddha figurine, or anything that helps you in your work.

## *The Table*

If you work as part of an organisation, you have no choice but to abide by their rules and regulations, so the size and placement of your table and the colour of your cloth will be dictated by those circumstances. However, if you are working on a less formal occasion, your stand or table decor is very personal. Some stands are witchy, some look like sets from The Lord of the Rings, and others are full of silk flowers, rainbows, fairies, Buddhas, angels, etc. It is a matter of personal preference.

## *The Fun of the Fair*

Fairs can be great fun because you work alongside others, and you will pick up many tips from the old hands. Some festivals have a wonderful atmosphere where everybody has a terrific time, but others encourage jealousy and irritating behaviour. Much of the atmosphere at these events is linked to their success, as it is a fact that if the stand holders make money, everybody is happy. If the event is a damp squib, tempers start to fray...

# 14: Do You Need Counselling Skills?

*'A great profession has grown up around counselling, but who listens to counsellors anyway?'*
JAMES WHALE - JOURNALIST

## *Training*

Telling other people how to live is a gratifying pastime, but is it counselling? If you truly wish to see yourself as a counsellor, look around to see what courses are available. Look into the time scale that the courses will take, see precisely what kind of studying or work will be required, and most importantly, take note of the charges. Find out what your qualifications will be when you have completed the course. When you think you have found the right course, ask if you can be put in touch with one or two people who have already completed it to give their opinion about it. If there is any hesitation over this, give the organisation second thoughts. If you can speak to a past student, ask them what they have got out of their course and whether they think it is good value. There may be impartial reviews online, so do an online search.

If you don't intend to get into heavy counselling, you don't need any training, but one thing you can do is to learn to listen, and by this, we mean really listening. Few people have the first idea of how to listen without jumping in with their two-pennyworth. In contrast, for many clients, talking to a sympathetic outsider who listens can give them more spiritual and mental healing than anything else. The other important factor is not to be unduly pessimistic. It's easier to highlight negative rather than positive issues, but that can harm the client, who relies on you for a balanced viewpoint.

Please remember that you cannot put someone's life right in an hour. Suppose a client consults a professional counsellor or psychotherapist. In that case, this will involve many appointments taken over a period of time, along with exercises, homework, and perhaps group therapy, as part of the package. You can't be expected to obtain the same results in a one-off reading. Sometimes all you can do is open your client's mind to fresh ways of thinking and suggest they seek a qualified counsellor for further help. If you know someone who you think can help your client and who is happy to receive referrals, pass their details on.

### An Astrologer's View

Without negating my comments in the previous paragraph - because the following tale is an extreme example - Jan and I remember seeing a very interesting article in an American astrology magazine, written by a man who was obviously a sensitive and intelligent astrologer. He said that he had clients who had been in therapy for months or even years at considerable expense to themselves. He cited one case where the psychoanalyst took over eighteen months to work out the matter with his client. Astrologers must determine what is bothering the client and how things will work out in the future, and they must do so within a couple of hours - and for a minuscule fraction of the money a psycho-analyst can expect to earn.

This is not to tarnish the name of psychoanalysis because not every psychoanalyst takes eighteen months to work out his client's problem, and sometimes the kind of time-consuming techniques therapists and analysts use are exactly what the client needs. Sometimes a twelve-step programme with Alcoholics Anonymous or some other such organisation is required. However, this just goes to show what the general public expects of us and the high standards that we expect of ourselves.

Strictly speaking, the answer to whether you should give counselling as part of your job is that you will do what comes naturally to you. Some highly successful psychic Consultants give absolutely no advice or help, seeing their job as passing on the information they are given by their spirit guides and then leaving it at that. Others do try to help, with varying amounts of success.

### *Specific Advice*

Clients will sometimes face you with problems outside your sphere of expertise. Such problems could be medical, legal, financial or other matters requiring specialist knowledge. You can only give such a client the information at your disposal and only if you are absolutely sure of what you see. You can make reasonably encouraging remarks if you think the client will come out on the right side of whatever pickle they are in, but you must not get involved in giving advice in areas beyond your formal expertise.

If you suspect that one of your clients is harbouring an illness, gently suggest that they seek advice from a doctor just to put their mind at rest. In short, use your common sense and cover your back in any dodgy situation.

### *Sasha's Experiences*

Rex was a client who went on and on about some long-winded legal case, to the point where I decided that if I were a judge, I would find for the other side! Another client I will never forget had lost an absolute fortune due to having been a "Lloyd's Name". This is a special kind of insurance investment which had made a great deal of money for its investors in the past, but in the early 1990s, serious insurance losses, particularly in the asbestosis crisis, caused many of its investors to lose all their wealth and assets. My client was a Capricorn with strong Taurean qualities, so he needed wealth for the survival of his ego, and the poor man wanted me to provide him with sure-fire astrological stock-market advice so that he could gain back all his lost riches. I gently pointed out that if I could do this, I'd hardly be sitting in my back room giving readings for a living, as I would be rolling in money myself!

### *Soap Boxes*

You may be totally dedicated to some kind of alternative medicine or therapy that you simply can't help recommending. However, before you search for the brochure or phone number, please remember that many people prefer to find their own solutions. Your grateful client will doubtless drop your lovingly given piece of paper in the nearest trash can long before she arrives home. In my own case, the moment anyone suggests that I should buy some smelly concoction, I close my ears, as the only thing I want to drink when I am off-colour is a nice cup of tea.

Having said all the foregoing, if you have to offer some simple and practical advice, such as the phone number of a decent plumber, do pass it on by all means.

Readers usually have experience and common sense and find that some practical advice will often help a mildly confusing situation. The late Betty Nugent used to say that if the Reader is a medium channelling advice from a higher source, so much the better.

# 15: Things that Happen

If your motivation is to be seen as special, talking about your work to all and sundry might help, but whether this will make you a good Reader or Therapist is hard to judge. Here is a true story.

Several years ago, an acquaintance, who I will call Lionel, took up Tarot reading. Lionel had an aptitude for the cards, but his attitude was unusual because if a woman showed the slightest interest in the subject, he would take out his cards and lay them out for her. On one occasion, Lionel went to a local pub where he found an attractive barmaid working behind the bar. He whipped out his cards and spread them out on the bar to give the busy barmaid a reading, and she strained to listen to what he was saying while at the same time serving her other customers. The pub happened to be in a business area, so the clientele mainly consisted of men, and Lionel was in seventh heaven because he was achieving a lifetime ambition of capturing the wholehearted attention of an attractive female while making other men wait around for her to attend to them. He became so overwhelmed with the success of this ploy that the following week he pulled out his cards at the supermarket checkout - causing even more chaos!

## *Saying No*

In party or social situations, you will encounter several responses when people discover what you do. Some people will be happy to ask a few intelligent questions and leave it at that, while others will press you for an on-the-spot reading or for you to give them some therapy there and then. Some will even try to goad you into proving yourself by insinuating that you aren't any good. When I was a full-time Reader and out on social events that had nothing to do with my job, I found it easier to say I was a secretary than to tell anybody what I really did.

The late Jonathan Dee told me that whenever he was out, someone would invariably stick his hand under Jon's nose, expecting him to read it, even though Jonathan was an astrologer and not a palmist. Most people think we all read hands, regardless.

A couple of decades ago, I went to South Africa to stay with my friend Vivien, and the first thing we did after my long journey was to sit in Viv's garden, enjoying a cuppa and a catch-up gossip. To my astonishment, a young woman climbed over the wall at the back of Viv's garden and approached me. She sat down and demanded that I read her cards. Vivien tried to explain that I had been travelling for nearly twenty-four hours and was exhausted and anyway, I wasn't at work at the time. Nevertheless, the young woman insisted that I unpack my Tarot cards and give her a reading. Nothing that Vivien or I said seemed to penetrate. I was too worn out from my journey to put up with this, so I told the girl to leave and made it clear in no uncertain terms that nothing on earth would induce me to give her a reading – not then and not ever!

If you are out socially, you are entitled to spend your free time enjoying yourself. Sometimes you may be perfectly happy to talk about your work, but if you don't feel like it, don't do it.

## *The Marine Bandsman Syndrome*

I remember one lovely lady who came to me for a reading to discover whether her dying relationship with a marine bandsman could be saved. Sadly, I confirmed that her fears were correct and that the affair was coming to an end. She wasn't surprised by the news but was understandably unhappy about it, though the main reason for her disappointment was unusual. Apparently, the lady had a deep and abiding urge to be a marine bandsman herself, but in those days, women were not accepted into the Marines or chosen to play in their bands. Also, the fact that she was female, shortish, plump and well into middle age was making this weird dream impossible, so she had done the next best thing, which was to sleep with a marine bandsman, but it just wasn't working out.

Most people reading this would write the lady off as a nutcase, but I concluded that it had something to do with a previous life situation, and I suggested that she look around for a regression therapist to take her back in time and find out why she was being driven demented by this strange desire.

Sadly, I never heard from her again, so I never found out whether she looked into her marine bandsman syndrome.

## *Hostility*

You will encounter hostile responses from some people, for several reasons; you may have the misfortune of talking to a religious fundamentalist, which leaves you with two choices. You could ask them to explain their beliefs and try to convince you about their beliefs, or you could excuse yourself, find a wickedly large drink and turn away and chat with someone more likeable.

Apart from religious zealots, astronomers are the worst anti-astrology folk I have ever encountered. Most (not all) are dreadful bigots, and the one good thing about them is that there aren't many of them. Unlike us, many astronomers tend to be amateurs who often fancy themselves as scientists and thus consider themselves special.

Some sociologists can also be hostile, but anybody in the counselling business is likely to be on our side, as their work borders on our own and, in some cases, is the same as ours. These comments are generalisations, though, because civilians can be hostile, accepting or anything else, depending upon their natures. I have found sympathetic meteorologists, financial analysts, police officers, bank managers, business executives and even some astronomers who are also closet astrologers and clairvoyants.

Some civilians are jealous of our talents, while many think we earn a fortune from weak-minded people who pay enormous sums to consult us. I remember one occasion when an accountant lectured me on the fact that I should be giving my time and skills away for nothing, but I said that when he used his training and his expensive office to give free accountancy to his clients, I might consider doing the same.

It can be unwise to do business on a social occasion, so if someone shows a genuine interest in consulting you, just hand them a business card and tell them to ring you to discuss details.

## *Take a Break*

Do things unrelated to your work to create a balance in your life, so take the time to socialise, relax and do something you enjoy

# 16: Health and Safety

Jan and I are the last people on earth to lecture people on health matters because we sit for long hours at our computers and sometimes forget to eat properly. However, there are a few sensible steps we all should take. The first thing to remember is that as a self-employed person, when you are ill, you can't work, and if you can't work, you can't earn money, so you must try to look after your health as best as you can. Today's world is flooded with health information, so you should find the answers to your health problems, but some issues don't affect those who have reliable jobs, such as:

- The financial uncertainty of living with a fluctuating income.
- Long or irregular hours of work.
- Living "over the shop" and not really being able to get away from work.
- The loneliness factor or spending too much time at home.
- Dealing with many people who have problems.
- Not being able to judge your own performance.

## *Stress in the Workplace*
We once read an interesting article about this, and the answer was that most stress comes not from the job itself but from those one has to work with – or for – in many cases. Feelings of powerless, rage, hopelessness, lack of appreciation, being treated disrespectfully and other stresses of this kind can make any job a nightmare, whereas even a truly challenging job can be enjoyable if the employee is appreciated. Too many people dread going to work and struggle to shake off their negative feelings even when they are away from the job. Self-employment solves this problem

at a stroke, and as long as you enjoy your work, you should be much happier than a troubled employee would be.

## *Financial Uncertainty*

A number of the chapters in this book deal with financial matters; if you take the advice on board, you should be able to avoid some financial stresses. The following advice list sums up a few simple steps that should help:

- If you need a regular income, do something other than rely on your consultancy. Make this job as different from consultancy work as possible so that it creates a balance.
- Always put away part of your income so you have some savings for a rainy day.
- Keep good records so your tax bill doesn't come as a nasty shock.
- Stay away from debt, and don't buy things you can't afford or don't need.
- Don't give away your savings to the first scrounger who asks for money.
- Spread the load by varying your work, so give lectures, write articles or do anything else that brings in a little money from a different source.

## *Hours of Work*

Try not to become so involved with your work that it becomes all-consuming. If you become successful, your clients will pester you for appointments, but it is a poor policy to work too many hours. Clients want to visit you when they fancy it, and you can end up with appointments scattered throughout the week, breaking up each day and preventing you from taking a proper rest. Work out a schedule of the hours that suit your lifestyle and build in breaks where you do something different. Don't just use your off days to catch up on housework or other chores but designate time to visit friends and family, go on outings, or simply laze around and rest.

Depending upon how much you need to work, you may have to see some clients in the evenings or at weekends. Don't fill up every weekend with appointments unless you prefer to take your days off during the week. Establishing a rhythm that suits you will take time, but the main thing is not to allow clients to bully you into seeing them on your days off. If you need a catnap to get through the day, build in time for this and don't feel guilty about it. Now and then, stop and count up the hours you spend working, including any chores related to your business, such as doing the bookkeeping or buying equipment for your work. If your consultancy has taken off and the hours you are working are becoming ridiculous, consider raising your prices, as this will bring you in more money during fewer hours of work and bring in a better type of client.

Allow times during your working day for a break so that you can get something to eat and drink. If you want to walk around the block or sit and read a newspaper for half an hour, do so. In short, don't work yourself to death unless you are in dire financial straits.

## *Too Many People With Problems*

Healers and workers in the psychic arena pick up on the misery or neuroticism surrounding us during our working day, which can cling to us afterwards if we are not careful. We can't always help our clients as much as we want, so we can even feel guilty about our limitations. Just as police officers can end up assuming that most people are crooks, we can conclude that most people are crazy. It helps if we can get away from the work scene occasionally, but friends who also work in our field are often helpful, as they can share their experiences with us, making us feel less alone or inadequate. Friends also help us to see the funny side of things.

## *Psychic Self-Defence*

Psychic self-defence techniques are useful in every walk of life, but in ours, they are invaluable. First, you should clear your aura at the end of each working day. The method that I describe here was passed on to me by Eve Bingham. Imagine clean, clear water coming down from the universe, entering the top of your head, rushing through your body and out through the extremities. Once you have done this, close down each one of your chakra centres and do no more esoteric work for the rest of the day.

### *How to close your chakras*
Imagine that your body is filled with a bright white light that reaches miles up into the air until it is attached to the universe above you, and this light also reaches miles into the earth below you.

- Turn off that section of the light that is beneath your feet.
- Draw the light up your legs, leaving them in darkness.
- Imagine a red glow at the base of your trunk, and then simply turn this red glowing light off.
- Draw the darkness of night upwards through your body until the white light only reaches as far as the middle of your abdomen.
- Imagine an orange glow in the middle of your abdomen, then close this down.
- Draw the darkness of night upwards once again until your body is only lighted down as far as your diaphragm, and then imagine a glowing yellow light there. Turn the yellow light off.
- Draw the darkness upwards from your diaphragm to the middle of your chest and imagine a glowing, green light there. Turn the green light off.
- Draw the darkness upwards from your chest area to your throat, cloaked in a light blue, glowing light. Switch the blue light off.
- Draw the darkness up to the centre of your forehead, where you see a large dark blue eye. Close this eye down and ensure that it is completely shut.
- Now take the remaining white light up to the crown of your head, move it away to a point above your head, and then imagine an amethyst water lily there (a lotus flower). Close this flower down tightly.
- Send the remaining light up, up and away to the universe.

If you need to open your chakras before working, meditating, or for any other spiritual purpose, simply reverse this procedure.

It is also a good idea to take frequent showers and wash your hair, as this will help keep the psychic and emotional residue out of your aura. It is a fact that those who work in our field are the cleanest people on earth because we shower and bathe so often!

### *Serious Self-Defence*

You may be placed under some kind of psychic attack at some point in your life due to being among people who are jealous, spiteful, malicious, unkind and insensitive. You can treat this much of the time by simply imagining yourself encased in a mirrored egg or a gleaming suit of armour because the bright shine will reflect the unpleasantness and negativity away from you and send it back to the perpetrators.

Once in a very blue moon, a Reader will find him or herself under a genuinely nasty psychic attack from people who know how to bring others down. The worst of all scenarios is where some kind of malicious spirit is blocking you, and in this case, you will have to find a good clearance expert and have the darn thing exorcised! It will be well worth it if this takes the whole gamut of bell, book, candle, holy water, and a pricey fee.

If you think a spiritual force is bugging your place of business, a quick method of clearing this is to open your chakras and imagine the malignant spirit being taken away up into the light. After you have done this, use your imagination to fill the space with clean, clear pale blue water from the ground up to the roof, as this will prevent the malignant force from returning. Finally, ask your god or gods to bless the location and for it to be a peaceful and prosperous place for you to work in. If the situation continues or there are any poltergeists or other psychic phenomena you are not happy about, call in a team of exorcising mediums to clear it.

At this point in our ruminations, Jan and I have asked ourselves how many other business books advise people to clear themselves or their place of work of spiritual mischief or, better still, to call in an exorcist! Jan spent thirty-one years in banking before getting involved in the intricacies of the psychic world, but now he has seen enough of the spiritual world to understand what can happen. The preceding ideas might appear potty, but they are not so daft when we consider that people in Oriental countries call in Feng Shui experts before opening a new business, especially in banking or other large enterprises.

### *What if all the other Readers are better than I am?*

Feelings of doubt occasionally assail us, and the certainty that other Readers are better than we are ourselves can sap our confidence. The best approach is to look at the results of your own work and to consider whether your clients are happy with what you are doing for them. If your clients are satisfied, that is all that matters, so just be yourself and get on with the job in your own way. The following comments may help you to put this problem into perspective.

Unless you actually see your fellow Readers at work, all you have to go on is what they tell you, and human nature is such that they will inevitably boast about their successes. If a Reader does tell you about a failed reading, then this is likely to be put down to the fact that "the client was in denial and refused to accept anything that was said to him".

Also, remember that Readers vary a great deal in their approach, and clients also vary a great deal. The chances are that a more forthright and confident Reader who thinks they know it all or likes to hector a client "for his or her own good" won't necessarily please a sensitive or nervy client half as much as a more diffident, careful type of Reader would. Even if you see other Readers at work and find them impressive, remember that you can't see yourself at work, making it impossible to judge your own performance. Also, remember that we all have good and bad days, and you may be seeing another Reader at a time when their "form" is at its best. They are probably not half as good the rest of the time.

# 17: Legal and Official Matters

## *Income Tax*

One astrologer told us of a case of a therapist who was recently investigated in minute detail by the tax department. The tax inspector looked over this guy's books right back over six years, and he also asked to see the therapist's diaries for those years to match the number of appointments to the money the man had paid into his business account in the bank. As it happened, the taxman was satisfied that the therapist had done all the right things, which was the end of the matter, but it was an unpleasant and extremely stressful experience. Other Readers in our field suggest that the tax people are suspicious of us because we handle cash, and they feel that we must be earning much more than we are declaring. Our experience with the tax inspectors is that when they see the reality of how hard we work and what we earn, they wonder how we manage to live! The answer, as always, is to keep all receipts for anything you buy that relates to your business, to declare your earnings and then either get help from the tax office or use a good accountant when it comes to filling in forms and suchlike.

## *Legal Problems*

You will have noticed how on the copyright page of this book, we have used a disclaimer; originally just for the US market, but there have been developments that make a disclaimer essential here in the UK and the EU as well.

Even in Britain, some clients will sue a Reader for an unsatisfactory reading. And EU legislation (that still applies in the UK after Brexit) gives a client additional protection against fraudulent Readers. Well and good, but the legislation places unreasonably high demands on genuine Readers, opening them up to frivolous demands from streetwise clients.

## *Commercial Insurance*

Sign up for Public Liability and Professional Indemnity insurance to protect you from most business hazards. It nay seem an unnecessary expense, but consultants have been successful sued for many thousands of pounds. Don't risk it.

# 18: Readings in Action

Here are a few stories that I have gathered over the years.

### The Afflicted Neptune
My lovely late friend, Jonathan Dee, told me about the day he was analysing a client's chart and noticed that the client had an "afflicted" Neptune in the fourth house. The fourth house represents the past, often the home and family environment and sometimes one of the parents, while Neptune indicates water or alcohol.

Jonathan casually asked his client, "Was your father, by any chance, a drunken sailor?" "No," answered the client, "he was a drunken swimming pool attendant!"

### The Bad Leg Case
I was working at a busy psychic fair in London and reading one set of hands after another when a middle-aged man turned up, whose fingernails on the left hand suggested he had suffered considerable damage to his left leg. After a while, I looked up at the client and told him what I had seen. The client casually leaned down, picked up a stick that I hadn't noticed and without saying a word, hit the stick against his left leg, which promptly gave off a decidedly metallic bong. I gazed at the laughing client in astonishment as he told me he had lost his leg many years before in a motorcycle accident.

### Don't Make Assumptions
The late Malcolm Wright told a tale of the day he was giving readings at a busy festival when a lady in a wheelchair was pushed up to him so he could give her a reading. The poor woman had apparently been very badly crippled and generally deformed

from birth, but Malcolm proceeded to read her hand, and he was astonished to find a full life written there. The client confirmed that she was happily married with three lovely children. Malcolm was amazed to see a person in such a state with such a normal lifestyle, but there it was, written in her hands for all to see! The moral of this story is to read what is on the hands rather than making assumptions.

### The Three Women

While Sasha was busy lecturing in South Africa, she couldn't help being fascinated by three beautiful and well-dressed women sitting close to the front of the room. After her talk, a few people, including the three women, asked her to read their hands. Sasha was astonished to find that all three of these glamorous ladies were transgender people who had started life as men, but she gave them their reading as women because, clearly, that is what they had become.

### The Wannabe Accountant

Psychic fairs can attract their fair share of nutcases, and this was one of them.

A skinny young Indian man gave Sasha his hands to read, and she immediately spotted the kind of irregularities on the headline that showed all was far from well with this man on a mental level. After she had given the man a somewhat generalised reading, he told her that he was out of work but that he was determined to become an accountant, and he asked her when this was likely to happen. It flashed through Sasha's mind that the poor chap had more chance of winning an Olympic gold medal than of tackling something that required as much self-discipline and intelligence as accountancy, so she told him she couldn't see him becoming an accountant and that perhaps he should lower his sights a little. The man went ballistic and clearly showed the strange cast of his broken mind, but Sasha smiled and shrugged as he stomped off to ask the organisers for his money back. When the Readers got together for a chat after the festival, Sasha discovered that this man had been to one Reader after another, and all of them had told him exactly the same thing, and all had experienced the same result.

## *Nostradamus*

Jan and Sasha received a package in the post from a man in New Zealand who was trying to get a book published. The pages were part of an introduction to a carefully worked treatise on the date for the potential end of the world. As Sasha and Jan checked through the dense and heavily academic tract, they became so impressed with the approach's sources, arguments and sheer intellectualism that they began to think the author had a point. However, before they became too concerned about the world's impending end, they noticed the date that the world was due to end had already passed while the package was on its way from New Zealand...

A similar story was of an author who wrote books showing how the world would end in 2012, owing to this being the end of the Mayan calendar or some such thing.

As astrologers, we know that Pluto entering Aquarius will bring significant changes to the world, but we are reluctant to predict the end of the world or anything depressing because so many have done so in the past, and we're all still here. Anyway, even if the world does end, there isn't much we can do about it, so it isn't worth worrying about.

## *A Chance to Boast*

Sasha was reading hands at a busy festival when she became aware that an important journey was marked on one particular lady client's hands. The line pointed towards Canada as a likely destination. The lady confirmed that she had been to Canada. The line had a peculiar mark about three-quarters of the way along its length, and in a moment of inspiration, Sasha suggested that the lady was going to Toronto - this city being about three-quarters along the map of Canada from the western edge. This, too, was confirmed. A tiny line ran up and down through this mark and just off to the left of the line, and for all the world, like a turning off the main road, she could see another tiny line. As it happens, Sasha had been to Toronto, and she knew that the main road that ran north and south through the town was Yonge Street. Hence, she suggested to her client that the exact destination was a turning or two up from the Eaton Centre on the left-hand side of Yonge

Street. The astonished client also confirmed this, and she and Sasha gazed at each other in amazement!

The moral of this story is that we sometimes get things right!

### *Full House*

On this particular day, the first few cards that emerged from the pack were four aces and the Fool. Sasha suggested that the client was about to make a significant change and that almost every reference point in her life was about to vanish and be replaced by something completely different. Some years later, the client returned for another reading, and it appeared that this lady had thrown up her job, sold her house, and left to work in a hospital in Africa. She had met a doctor at the hospital who became the love of her life; they were getting married and going to live permanently in Africa.

This also shows that we sometimes get things right!

### *Road Signs*

One day, Sasha was busy giving short Tarot readings over a phone line on a radio station in the south of England when a man came on the line. Sasha threw out a few cards for him, and she soon saw an image in her mind's eye of the man driving along the M4 motorway in heavy rain while crying his heart out. She could even see the road signs passing by on the left. She told her listener what she saw, and he told her a strange tale. Apparently, he had insisted on giving up his job in London and relocating his family to the west country, but he had done this without enough forethought and without giving due consideration to his wife or asking her opinion about the move. The property he had bought turned out to be a water-logged wreck, and there was no possibility of work for himself or his wife in the area. She had walked out in disgust, returned to London with the children and started divorce proceedings.

### *Candle in the Wind*

Early in 1984, Sasha attended a talk and demonstration by Dave Bingham of the British Astrological and Psychic Society. On this occasion, Dave was demonstrating the ancient art of candle scrying. The idea is to light a candle, relax and gaze into its flame until visions begin to come. As Dave started to talk about what he could "see", Sasha concentrated absent-mindedly upon Dave, and within a moment or two, she also began to see visions. Suddenly both Sasha and Dave found themselves seeing a coach trip to Venice. Nothing was further from Sasha's mind at that time, but a few weeks later, the strangest thing happened.

Before this, one of Sasha's regular clients had come to her for an astrology reading, asking for advice about a job he was considering. Sasha used straightforward astrology for this and concluded that the job had something to do with travel. Then, her intuition kicked in, and she told him he would take a job as a travel representative or courier, escorting people on tours around the UK. She felt he would only work in the UK and not Europe, and she could see this factor as important.

Robert then told Sasha that he had agreed to take a job with a firm that took groups of American students around the UK but that this firm had a prior booking to take a group around Europe, and they didn't have anybody on hand to escort the group. The man had told Sasha's client that if he wanted the job, he must either escort this group himself or find someone else. Without thinking, Sasha's mouth opened, and she commented that she could probably do the job because she spoke several languages, had travelled a lot and knew most European countries' history, geography and conditions. After the client had gone, Sasha forgot all about the reading and her throw-away comment until a month later when her client rang her and told her it was all fixed up and that "her group" would be arriving at Heathrow Airport in a couple of days' time. The money was good, and Sasha felt she couldn't turn this offer down.

The group arrived, and it turned out that they were a group of youngsters from a University, and they had a series of singing engagements in various parts of Europe, including Venice. Sasha did the job, returned with some much-needed money and had a great time into the bargain - especially in Venice, which was the only place on the trip where the torrential rain that dogged the tour had ceased and the sun had come out. Dave's prediction had been spot on!

## There's Gold in Them Thar Hills

Sasha was giving a phone-in reading at a radio station, and she was talking to a man who she felt convinced would go abroad and dig for gold. This crazy idea was followed in her mind's eye by a vision of the man actually digging up a large nugget of the stuff and becoming rich. This seemed such a ludicrous idea that although she told the man and the listening audience what she had seen, she laughed it off and forgot all about it. A year later, Sasha was back at the same radio station, giving readings on the same programme, when the "gold" man phoned in again. Apparently, he had travelled to South America, staked a claim, struck gold, and was now rich!

## *Murder Most Foul*

Some years ago, after doing one of her regular radio programmes, a young woman who worked at the radio station begged Sasha to stay on after the show to help her. It turned out that the girl's brother had gone to Northern Ireland and had later turned up dead in a wood. The girl knew her brother had been killed, but nobody knew who had done the deed or why it had happened. The Irish police had assumed it was something to do with the troubles that afflicted the area at the time and that the young Englishman had been mistaken for someone else. The only odd thing was that the man had been stabbed to death, apparently an unusual form of murder in that time and place.

Sasha tuned in and immediately "saw" the young lady's brother at the edge of the woods, and she then she saw him arguing furiously with another young man. The second man lost his temper, took out a knife and repeatedly stabbed her brother. As Sasha concentrated on the emotions inherent in the scene, she became convinced that this was nothing to do with the Irish troubles but jealousy over the poaching of the murderer's girlfriend by the brother. The tearful young lady said that was quite possible because her brother had been a handsome lad and had been fond of pinching other men's women as a rather nasty macho game. This time the game had clearly gone very wrong.

***

So, there we are… A very good psychic called Carina once told me, "What we see are not whole pictures but shadows, and we have to interpret what we can from them, which isn't easy."

# 19: Writing

*Read over your compositions, and wherever you meet with a passage which you think is particularly fine, strike it out.*
SAMUEL JOHNSON QUOTING A COLLEGE TUTOR. 30TH APRIL 1773.

## Magazines

If somebody calls you and says they are from XYZ magazine, find out whether this is true. Many enquiries will be from freelance writers who are hoping to sell articles to a magazine. They may take your work and pass it off as theirs, including taking the fee for the job. Phone the magazine itself and ask about this if you are in any doubt. If the job looks "kosher", find out the following before agreeing to anything:

* Exactly what they want you to write about and how many words they want.
* The deadline.
* How they want the work submitted.
* Whether they need illustrations and in what form.
* Whether you are the only contributor to the article or if you are one of a number.
* Whether your name is going to be printed alongside your article.
* Whether the article is likely to be changed much.
* The payment terms, including how much and when they intend to pay.

Always send an "immediate payment' invoice with your work, although many organisations pay their invoices monthly, and if this is not paid after 30 days, chase the invoice through the magazine's accounts department. You may have to send a copy invoice because editors sometimes forget to forward invoices to the accounts department.

### *Important Tips*
The copyright of your work should remain with you, but you can't reuse exactly the same article in another publication.

### *Writing a Stars Column*
A stars column is great exposure for any astrologer, but it is hard work, and you have to balance the time it will take against the income that this will bring. In my experience, the rate in some cases is laughable and at others very good indeed. Some publications paid on the nail, and others had to be chased. Contact other contributors to the publication and see what their experience is like.

### *Phone Lines*
If you are asked to record a phone line for a paper or a magazine, be very careful how you negotiate this. Find out precisely what the work will entail, what you will be paid, and when.

### *Books*
Many years ago, an excellent editor called Simon Franklin told me the issues that made him immediately reject a manuscript, and here they are in Simon's own words:

- We already have books on that subject in our list.
- The idea is too specialised to appeal to a reasonably broad readership.
- The manuscript is so poorly written and disorganised that it needs to be rewritten.
- The proffered manuscript had been channelled by a little man in a flying saucer.

After decades in the publishing business, Jan and I couldn't say it better.

## *Books*

If you want to know how to write a book, buy our small paperback or Kindle ebook called "Self-Publishing with Stellium". It works for those who want to be conventionally published or self-published, and answers most new authors' questions.

Treat yourself to a copy of "The Writers and Artists Year Book" (in the USA, buy "The Writer's Market"). From this, you can identify the publishers who produce the book genre(s) that you write about. Look on the publishers' websites to see what each publisher wants, which will likely be a synopsis, some sample material, and perhaps a little information about yourself. Nowadays, you will usually submit the information by email, but if a hard copy is required, don't forget to enclose a stamped addressed envelope if you want your content to be returned to you.

If you hear nothing from a publisher after about six weeks, ring them. If your book is rejected, don't let this get you down. Some years ago, I read that it is bad form to send the same book outline to more than one publisher at the same time. This is complete rubbish, so send your material to everybody, typically by email.

If you don't get anywhere, contact us and get the book self-published by our sister company, Stellium Ltd. Please note that you are entitled to have your work out in the wide world, but we draw the line at rants, pornography, racism, other misguided content or incredibly badly writing. Self-publishing isn't the bad thing it used to be, it doesn't cost much, and your work will be "out there" rather than languishing in a bottom drawer somewhere. In some cases, if it attracts public appeal, a self-pub book can also be taken up for conventional publishing.

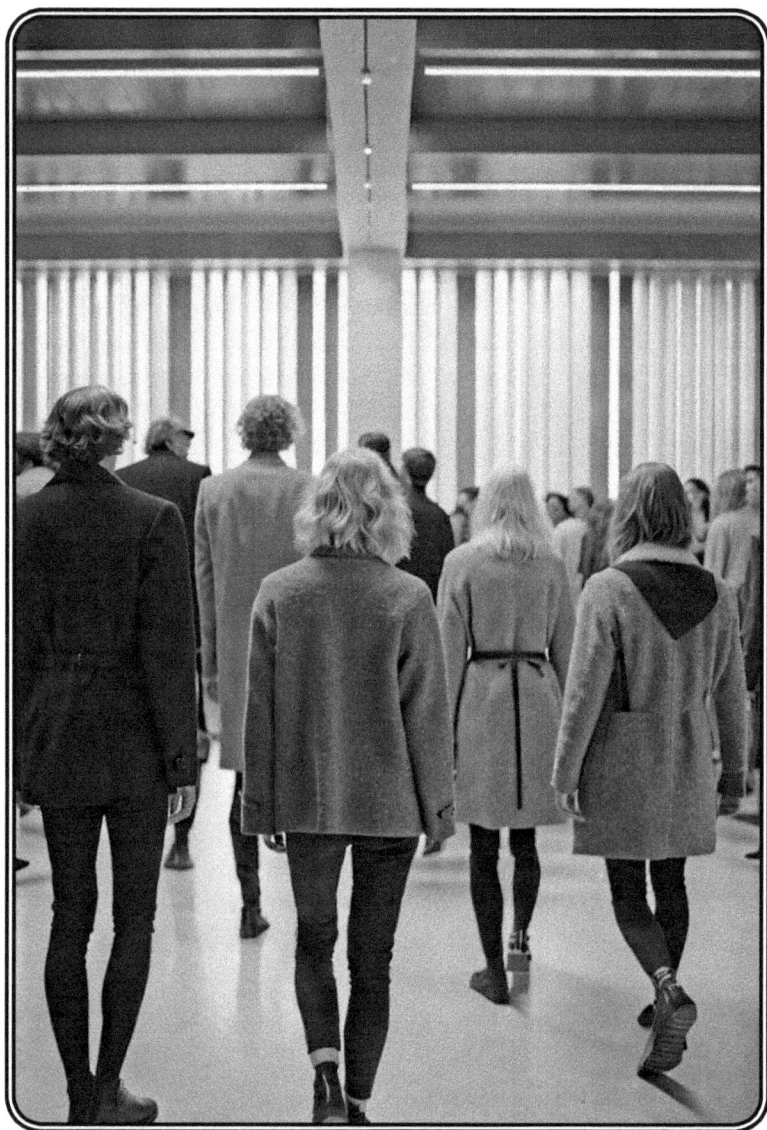

# 20: Conclusion

Jan and I hope the advice, suggestions and stories in this book help you on the road to a successful career. You may never become rich but you will enjoy your work, and there is a lot to be said for that.

We both wish you the very best of luck in your new career!
Sasha and Jan

# Index

# Index

www.ingramcontent.com/pod-product-compliance
Lightning Source LLC
Chambersburg PA
CBHW050821090426
42737CB00022B/3464